YOUR FIRST HOME

THE PROVEN PATH
TO HOME OWNERSHIP

A KELLER WILLIAMS® REALTY GUIDE

GARY KELLER

WITH DAVE JENKS AND JAY PAPASAN

ISBN: 978-1-932649-15-4

This publication is designed to provide accurate and authoritative information in regard to the subject matter covered. It is sold with the understanding that neither the author nor the publisher is engaged in rendering legal, accounting, or other professional service. If legal advice or other expert assistance is required, the services of a competent professional person should be sought.

> — From a Declaration of Principles jointly adopted by a Committee
> of the American Bar Association and a Committee of Publishers

This book is printed on 30 percent post-consumer recycled, acid-free paper. The authors and Rellek Publishing Partners, Ltd., are committed to sustainable printing practices, which include the use of recycled and acid-free paper whenever available.

First Edition

Current printing: March 2016

OUR MISSION

We at Keller Williams Realty love real estate—the land, the homes and all those involved in the purchase, ownership, and sale of it. Professionally, we are dedicated to discovering and sharing the best real estate wisdom, practices, and models with everyone. The insights in this guide come from real-life experiences of hundreds of thousands of first-time home buyers with whom we have worked. In addition, our team has undertaken more than a decade of continuous in-depth research on all the steps, facets, and nuances of the home-buying process. We are excited to share this collective wisdom for the benefit of all those who are seeking to buy their first home and experience the rewards of home ownership.

OUR BELIEF

We believe that home ownership sits at the core of a free-enterprise economy and a nation of opportunity. It is a statement not only of personal freedom but also of financial strength. Beyond this, we believe in an even more fundamental truth: there is no place like home. From childhood to parenthood to retirement, your home represents an ever-present source of incredible emotional strength—it is, in fact, where your heart is.

CONTENTS

· · · · ·

PREFACE

. . . . .

I can still remember buying my first home—it was a big deal in my life. I loved that home, but funny thing is, it was actually my second choice. My first choice slipped away from me. It wasn't anyone's fault but mine. I found it, but instead of buying it, I drove by it every day, dreaming about living there. Certain of my desire, I was uncertain of the market and my next move. Unfortunately, and to my horror, the fifth day I drove by, it had a sold sign on it. I was heartbroken but, now certain about what to do, immediately drove over and bought my second choice.

The reason I share this with you is that even as an experienced real estate agent, I lost the first home I ever wanted, and I don't want the same thing to happen to you. It is also important to keep in mind that your first home probably won't be your last home. However, making that first purchase paves the way to owning your ultimate dream home faster than you think. As my father, Lew Keller, told me when buying my first home, "Buy it to sell it."

This book is about buying your first home, and I want to encourage you to make that leap. Owning a home will not only lay a solid foundation for your financial future but will also set the tone for your own personal lifestyle. It truly enables you to live the ultimate dream. And while it may quite possibly be the most expensive investment you've ever made, it will also be one of the smartest.

The process of buying your first home—from writing an offer to financing the purchase to navigating the closing—can be downright confusing. You're going to have a lot of questions, and not knowing all the answers can be stressful, but I can guarantee you one thing: it's absolutely worth the effort.

This book's goal is to help you know what to expect and be your trusted reference guide. I encourage you to skip around—this isn't a textbook or a "home" work assignment. Dig into the parts that interest you, and skim over those that don't. But first, let me share the most important piece of advice we can give you: you don't need to know everything.

With three decades of experience as a real estate agent and business owner, I've had a hand in literally thousands of real estate transactions. You know what? I still don't know everything. And I don't want to know everything! Knowing it all, I've found, isn't nearly as important as knowing who you can count on for expert advice. I'm proud to depend on the skills and talents of the people I work with, and that's what I would encourage you to do when you're out there looking for your first home.

Remember, your real estate agent and mortgage lender already know the nuts and bolts. They are market and transaction experts who will be able to answer your questions—if they can't, they'll find someone who can. But there are some questions that only you can answer: Where do I want to live? What does my ideal home look like? How much can I comfortably afford? Does this home purchase meet my family's needs, and fit our long-term plans? These are the questions that require your serious focus and sincere answers.

Real estate agents will tell you that helping first-time home buyers is one of the most satisfying aspects of their work. They know that becoming a home owner is a huge milestone, and they feel honored to be involved. It's an exciting opportunity, an emotional moment that means so many powerful things: I've arrived. I'm responsible. We're secure. We're part of a neighborhood. We've realized the dream. We're home.

I love this business and am proud to help people take ownership of their first home. I have no doubt that whoever guides you through the weeks to come feels exactly the same way. So, good luck on your journey. I hope it's as smooth and enjoyable as it can be, and I know you'll be thrilled when you get there—into your first home.

Gary Keller
Cofounder and Chairman of the Board
Keller Williams Realty, Inc.

ACKNOWLEDGMENTS

· · · · ·

An incredible number of people across the United States and Canada shared their thoughts, time, and wisdom with us during the research and writing of this book. We would like to thank the following individuals we interviewed for their collaborative spirits and generosity: Debbie Abadie, Al Alba, Eric Anderson, Mo Anderson, Sherinne Anderson, Kerry Andrews, Ron Ario, Okie Arnot, Antonio Atacan, Georgine Atacan, Jennifer Barnes, Don Beach, Sylvie Begin, Rick Brash, JoAnna Breen, Jim Buff, Mark Bullard, Dennis Burkhardt, Jim Burr, Steve Chader, Marianne Collins, Eric Copper, Cheri Corrado, Peter Costa, John Davis, Adele DeMoro, Amy Denham, Lynda Dimond, Tom Draney, Karen Evans, Janet Faulk, Matthew Fetick, Nancy Field, Darrow Fiedler, John Furber, Gary Gentry, Sharon Gibbons, Ginger Gibson, Alisa Guido, Kalee Haley, Alisha Hall, Karen Halladay, Don Hamilton, Bruce Hardie, Joe Harker, Jill Heineck, Jeff Hooper, Lisa Jalufka, Steve Johns, Shannon Jones, Julissa Jumper, Joe Kazzoun, Karoline Kelsen, Garry Klassen, Dianna Kokoszka, Ron Kubek, Sherry Lewis, Tony Marin, Linda McKissack, Mike Mendoza, Chris Minteer, Zan Molko, Julie Nelson, Chris O'Keefe, David Osborn, Julie Pedraza, Carol Peyton, David Raesz, Linda Sabine, Rick Sergison, Elaine Sans Souci, Beverly Steiner, Mike Tavener, Ruth Taylor, Mary Tennant, Dave Tower, Ken Tuchtan, Nikki Ubaldini, Michelle Valigursky, Roy Van Winkle, and Mark Willis.

Writer Rachel Proctor May did a fabulous job of researching and putting the initial draft together. Jolynn Rogers also contributed her creative writing talents to the first-home experiences of our Keller Williams leaders.

We're indebted to the following financial professionals who took time away from more lucrative pursuits to talk us through the numbers: Barbara Frierson, Michael Hapke, Andra Morris, Sharon Neider, Tommy and Susan Nelms, Jack Nichols, Lisa Peters, Dawn Skinner, Mary Anne Stevens, and Larry Weisinger.

Home owners Jeffrey Barg, Rondell Bennett, Donna Corbin, Suzi Eskenazi, Datri Gasser, Amy Sue Graham, Kailey Humphries, Damir Markov, John and Elise McCaleb, Becky Pastner, Tonja Pitzer, Stanley and Wini Reben, Mark and Toni Tolerico, Teresa Van Horn, and Dawn Vaughn are also to be thanked for sharing with the world their personal stories of how they found that special first home.

An especially big thanks goes to Ann Glorioso and the generous staff at the Levittown Public Library for endowing the book with wonderful photography options. We're equally grateful to real estate associates Karen Barrington, Kim Bray, Kathy Leo, Evonne Montero, Heidi Greer Mosher, Julie Nelson, Pam Neske, Paula Perry, and Carol Peyton for taking photographs for the book.

To our crack publishing partners at Stonesong Press, Judy Linden and Ellen Scordato, who patiently worked with us for two years as we researched, developed, and originally brought the hardcover book to market, and to Mary Glenn at McGraw-Hill, who brought the paperback edition to the bookstores, we owe great thanks.

Finally, Rellek's exceptional writing, editing, research, and marketing team on this project—Julie Sherrier, Jonas Koffler, Mark McFarlane, Mary Keith Trawick, Suman Olney, Alice Nguyen, Maryanne Jordan, Jeffrey Ryder, Dawn Sroka, Annie Switt, Michael Balistreri, and Ellen Marks—took early drafts of *Your First Home* and made them shine. And our incomparable support team, Jeannine Abbott, Debi Bentley, Roxanne Chinn, Mindy Hager, Susan Mayfield, Teresa Metcalf, Allison Odom, Kellie Ramsay, Emily Schluter, and Valerie Vogler-Stipe. Thanks, team. You rock.

Gary Keller, Dave Jenks, and Jay Papasan

Visit us at YourFirstHomeBook.com for more information.

INTRODUCTION:
THERE'S NO PLACE LIKE HOME

• • • • •

HOME IS WHERE THE HEART IS

In 1948, Stanley and Wini Reben bought their first home for ninety dollars down. It was one of the many tiny two-bedroom Cape Cod homes springing up all over Levittown, New York, after World War II.

"I was thrilled," Wini remembers, more than half a century later. "After living in an apartment, those four rooms were like a palace."

The typical Cape Cod home of Levittown, New York, ca. 1948. Image courtesy of the Levittown Public Library collection.

Built at the astonishing rate of thirty a day, the homes in America's first planned community were small and affordable, often purchased with low-interest loans the government offered returning GIs. Stanley, who had just finished service in the Coast Guard, and Wini, who worked at a cosmetics counter at a local store, borrowed their down payment and occupied their $8,000 home before their street was even paved.

Levittown's 17,000 homes were built in an assembly-line fashion—they were identical on the inside and nearly so on the outside as well. In fact, a folk tune popularized by Pete Seeger in the 1960s dismissed planned communities like Levittown as "little boxes made of ticky-tacky" that "all looked just the same." But Stanley and Wini would tell you today that the home is defined by the homemaker, not the house itself. You see, the people who moved into the houses were all unique, with their own ideas about what makes a house a home.

The Rebens added a deck and finished the attic. Their neighbors added porches and gardens, bay windows, and dormers. Over the years, the fruit trees planted by the developers in each yard stretched their branches toward the sky, each taking a slightly different path. Fifty years later, when the Levittown Historical Society set out to purchase a home in its original condition, there were absolutely none to be found. All the once-identical houses had been individually transformed into homes as distinct as the people who lived in them.

And for those of you curious to know how much those 1948 homes later were selling for, a quick check of Levittown's real estate values revealed 2014 prices were just under $400,000 on average.

Your first home may come with jewel-toned carpets or solid-beige walls. It may be a challenging fixer-upper, a quaint old cottage, or a sleek modern. But from the moment you unpack your furniture and start hanging your pictures, your home becomes a mirror that reflects your taste and personality, your likes and dislikes, your values, and your dreams. It becomes yours because you make it yours.

The pride of ownership that comes with buying your first home is inevitable. Over the days and months to come, you will most likely create an environment of your very own—one that expresses your taste, style, and creativity. A home is also your haven—a place where you can be yourself and escape from the daily grind of the outside world. Once that front door is shut, you are free to be and do as you please.

A Levittown home today.
Image courtesy of the Levittown Public Library collection.

There is a special category of life's firsts. First kiss. Driving for the first time. Going away to college. Starting your first job. Saying, "I do." Having a child ... All these unique moments bring significance to the story of your life. Whether you're from Calgary, Cocoa Beach, or any place in between, walking into your own home for the first time is just as magical.

GARY'S FIRST HOME

When I was growing up, home had three different addresses in Houston, Texas. But some of my fondest memories are of my very first one, which was also my parents' first home. It was one of those sturdy tract houses you saw everywhere in the 1950s—three tiny bedrooms, two baths with shiny, pastel-colored tiles on the walls, a small den, and a tight two-car garage.

Our home stood on Dorothy Street, surrounded by others that were almost identical except for the color. The homes were separated by chain-link fences that kept the kids and pets safe but still freely invited conversations between neighbors. The lawns were all mowed and manicured. It was a great place to grow up. Looking back, I'm not surprised that the first house I wanted to buy— the one that got away—was the spitting image of that childhood home.

When I think of that house, so many heartfelt memories come crowding in. I recall my dad playing with us on the hardwood floor and tossing us up in the air. There was the huge swing set in the backyard. It wasn't one of those lightweight ones that rocks back and forth. Dad bought ours from a place that sold park playground equipment and then cemented it into the ground. It had swings, a slide, monkey bars, and even a trapeze, and it set the stage for many adventures. He also built a sandbox next to it, and my buddies and I spent hours there building tunnels and playing with our plastic cars and trucks. We built elaborate backyard forts, using cardboard boxes we scavenged from the nearby furniture store. Each summer Dad put up a blue plastic pool that would hold seven or eight kids. Everyone in the neighborhood congregated there.

I can still see my mother standing at the back fence and talking to our neighbor, Mrs. Ramsey, and my father, with a bandana around his head, mowing the lawn in his plaid shorts, dress shoes, and dark socks—dads didn't wear tennis shoes back then. I remember the cozy, wood-paneled breakfast nook with a Formica table where we gathered for meals, and where my mother once washed my mouth out with soap for saying something she thought was disrespectful. I recall birthdays and holidays, especially the aluminum Christmas tree with the color wheel—my two sisters and I spent hours watching the tree change colors as the wheel turned. Dad built a workshop in the backyard. He had someone pour the concrete foundation, and he constructed the rest. I carried his tools, and it was there I first learned how to hammer nails. Building the workshop took him a year, and although it was only 12 foot by 12 foot, I thought it was huge.

Buying your first home is probably the most exhilarating material experience you can have. Nothing else compares. It's where you hang your hat, where you rest your head; it's a source of security, an investment in your financial future. More importantly, a home becomes part of the psyche that houses your most powerful memories. You can reminisce about a rental, but you'll never love it the same way. Your home is where you build a workshop or cement a swing set into the ground or plant a rose garden like my dad and I did. There really is no place like home, especially when it's your own—and it's on Dorothy Street.

Gary Keller is cofounder and chairman of the board of Keller Williams Realty, Inc.

CHAPTER 1:
DECIDE TO BUY

• • • •

Having emigrated from the war-torn former Yugoslavia to Canada about twenty years ago, Damir Markov of Toronto, Ontario, recalls the decision to buy his own home as among the most important in his life. "Our home gave us a sense of security and stability, and a chance to build for our financial future. I'm very happy I chose to buy," says Damir.

Home is not only where your heart is, but it's also where your money is too. There are very few places you will treasure more than your home, and there are very few places you will have more treasure than in your home.

Although there are many good reasons for you to buy a home, wealth building ranks among thc top of the list. Imagine if Stanley and Wini had rented a home for fifty years instead of buying one. How would their lives be different? Without even trying to go through the whole list, the one fact that jumps out immediately is that they wouldn't own a home worth approximately $400,000— debt-free. For them, their home is not only where their heart is, it's where their wealth is too.

HOME IS WHERE YOUR WEALTH IS

Many people don't come to realize the importance of financial independence until later in their lives when they are faced with a personal or family circumstance that requires available money—a health situation, college tuition, the loss of a job, a needed purchase, or retirement. For many of these same people, they are relieved and grateful that they had purchased a home and built some financial wealth to draw on. They realized, in fact, that their home was the best investment they had ever made. And it saved the day.

Even beyond the ability to tap into your home's value is the oft-overlooked advantage of simply paying your home off, eliminating your monthly mortgage payment, and reducing your cost of living. For those who have experienced this in their lives, it is a liberating feeling.

For these reasons, we call home ownership the best "accidental investment" most people ever make. But, we believe when it is done right, as outlined in this book, home ownership becomes an "intentional investment" that lays the foundation for a life of financial security and personal choice.

There are solid financial reasons to support your decision to buy a home, and, among these, equity buildup, value appreciation, and tax benefits stand out. However, too often, people will talk themselves out of making one of the best financial decisions of their lives for reasons that when fully examined just don't make much sense. Listed here are the most common fears that might keep some first-time home buyers from making the transition from renter to home owner, along with the facts that will push you past them. Those who have the most fulfilling lives base their decisions on facts, not fears.

FEARS AND FACTS ABOUT BUYING YOUR FIRST HOME

Fear #1: I can't afford to buy a home now.

Fact: Actually, you can't afford not to buy a home now.

First, there is always a home you can afford to buy that will be a smart purchase for you—the only questions are what and where. If it's "what" that matters to you, then keep pushing out the "where" until you find it. If it's the "where" that matters to you, then keep narrowing your "what" until you find it. No matter what features it has or where it's located, there is always a good buy for you.

Second, if you are paying rent, you can afford to buy. From a financial point of view, in the United States, the tax savings on mortgage interest alone usually makes up most of the difference between rent and a mortgage payment.

Third, the earlier you buy, the earlier you will benefit from equity buildup and will be well-positioned for any future appreciation. The fact remains, the sooner and more seriously you begin the process of buying your home, the sooner you'll find the best buy for you.

**7 Fears About
Buying Your First Home**

1. I can't afford to buy a home now.
2. I should wait until the real estate market gets better.
3. I don't have money for the down payment.
4. I can't buy a home because my credit isn't very good.
5. I can't afford to buy my dream home.
6. I should wait to buy a home until I get married.
7. Buying a home seems way too complicated.

Fear # 2: I should wait until the real estate market gets better.

Fact: There is never a wrong time to buy the right home.

Historically, focusing on the market is never the smart approach to buying the right home. Whether right means the right price or the right property for you, waiting to time the market seldom works to your advantage. Trying to time the market in the short term is the easiest way to miss your timing for the long term. Keep in mind, it's the long-term factors that make real estate a solid investment. All you need to do in the short run is find a good buy (based on your needs and what is currently available) and make sure you have the financial ability to hold it for the long run. Once you've made this purchase, the long-term benefits of equity buildup, value appreciation, and tax benefits will always make it a right decision.

While you should always be aware of the fluctuations of local market conditions, real estate tends to be much more stable and rewarding over time than other types of investments. With the help of your real estate agent, you can find a home that meets your criteria and is a smart purchase in any market area and at any time. In the end, there are really only two ways to make money in real estate. You either hit the right timing of the market or you have enough time in the market. That is, you either happen upon the right moment to purchase your home or you hold it long enough for time to make your purchase right. If you miss the first, you most certainly can count on the second.

Fear # 3: I don't have money for the down payment.

Fact: There are a wide variety of down payment options available for you.

While many people believe that making a home purchase requires a substantial down payment, as much as 20 percent, this is seldom true. As a first-time buyer, options are always available to you that require much less than this number, some as low as 5 percent, some even less. Don't let the lack of a substantial down payment prevent you from investigating your home-purchasing opportunities.

There are many legitimate and sound financing options to choose from, and it only makes sense to investigate which one is right for you, your circumstances, and your pocketbook. And, by the way, delaying your purchase while trying to save up for your down payment will mean delaying all the financial benefits of home ownership. In other words, we think waiting could actually cost you money.

Fear # 4: I can't buy a home because my credit isn't very good.

Fact: A less-than-perfect credit score won't necessarily prevent you from buying a home.

Typically, there are two types of credit challenges—a poor credit history or no credit history. First, while it is valuable to have a good credit score, a poor one shouldn't prevent you from talking to several lenders to explore your options. You might be pleasantly surprised at the outcome. You can expect that a good loan officer (or mortgage specialist) will be able to help you resolve your credit challenges, often by simply showing you how to move or consolidate your debts, or by referring you to a credit counselor who will put you on a plan. Even though this plan may take a few months to implement, it immediately gets you on the path to ownership.

Another challenge is having no credit history because you are new to the workforce or have not made regular purchases on credit. In either case, there are still possible solutions that you will want to explore. One avenue for first-time home buyers is to secure financing with the help of a cosigner, such as a parent or a close relative, who is willing to stand by your ability to make the payments.

It's worth noting that there is no better way to improve or establish your credit rating than by having a mortgage and making timely payments.

Fear # 5: I can't afford to buy my dream home.

Fact: The best way to get closer to buying your dream home is to buy your first home.

Very few people can afford to buy their dream home when they buy their first home. In fact, according to the National Association of Realtors®, 67 percent of first-time home buyers in the United States compromised on some features of their first home. So you make some compromises, buy your first home, and start building equity. This approach takes you further and faster down the road to being able to own your dream home than if you hadn't purchased a home at all.

Gary Keller and his wife Mary serve as a great example of how this works. They used their first home as a forced savings plan for their future dream home. They even made additional principal payments when they could to accelerate their equity buildup. Interestingly, this approach allowed them to pay off their first home in about eight years. Then, all that financial equity was available to help them build a second home—their dream home.

Fear # 6: I should wait to buy a home until I get married.

Fact: There is no reason to wait.

When most people say they want to wait until they're married to buy their first home, what they're actually struggling with are two distinct issues: First, would it be better to wait until they had two incomes? And second, will my future spouse like the home I choose?

If marriage is not in your future, then neither of these issues matter and buying is the right decision. Putting off the decision to buy the right home is never the solution. Getting into the game as soon as possible is.

By the way, if marriage is in your future, then buying is also the right decision. If your future spouse doesn't like the home, you can rent it or sell it and use the proceeds along with your possible dual income to buy one you both like. If your spouse likes the home, problem solved.

The National Association of Realtors® reports that 30 percent of first-time U.S. home buyers are, in fact, single. They didn't wait, so why should you?

Fear # 7: Buying a home seems way too complicated.

Fact: Buying a home is way too complicated, but that's why you have help.

No one would ever tell you that buying a home is easy. It's not. That's why there is a team of professionals ready to guide you through the home-buying process every step of the way. From your real estate agent to your mortgage officer to the professional who handles your closing and everyone in between, these experts make a complex process simple for you.

Every year, hundreds of thousands of people buy their first home. In fact, over a third of all home buyers are first-time home buyers. So, why not you? After you experience the home-buying process the first time, you'll wonder why you didn't do it sooner.

Although many people begin this process with the self-defeating belief "I can't," those who step past their fears and buy their first home not only find "they can" but are also glad they did. We hope by now you realize that nothing should hold you back from buying your first home, but in case you're still on the fence or undecided, let's take a closer look at the most important financial reasons why you should buy.

THE BEAUTY OF BUILDING EQUITY

The U.S. Federal Reserve Board's Survey of Consumer Finances showed home owners had a median financial net worth of $195,400, while renters' net worth was just $5,400. (Net worth, by the way, is the best measure of wealth available. It is simply the dollar amount you get when you add up everything of value you own and subtract everything you currently owe.) Call it good planning or forced savings—either way, it works. A home is clearly the largest financial asset most people have, and this is because of the equity position they have in it.

So, just what is equity and what is its role in making home buying a smart financial decision? Equity is the portion of your home's value that you actually own. That is, it's the money that would go into your pocket after you sold it, paid off your mortgage, and handled any selling expenses.

AS YOU PAY OFF YOUR MORTGAGE, YOUR EQUITY GROWS

Sheila buys a $150,000 house with a $15,000 down payment (10 percent down) on a 30-year loan. As she makes regular monthly payments, she builds up her equity.

$135,000 DEBT
$15,000 EQUITY

Closing Day
Equity buildup begins

$75,000 DEBT
$75,000 EQUITY*

Year 22
Home is *half* paid off

$150,000 EQUITY*

Year 30
Home is paid off

*Not including equity gained through price appreciation

FIGURE 1.1

There are two ways to build equity in your home. The first is by paying down your mortgage. Unlike most purchases, when you buy a property, you're only required to pay part of the sales price up front. This is your down payment. For the remainder, you take out a loan that you agree to pay back in monthly installments over a period of years. This loan is called a mortgage loan because you're pledging your home as collateral—you have, in fact, mortgaged your home. A portion of these monthly mortgage payments applies toward principal (the original amount you borrowed), and the other portion goes toward interest (the cost of the loan). Over time, as you pay back the principal, you gradually start to own more and more of the home's value. In other words, you build up equity.

As Figure 1.1 indicates, many people are surprised that on a thirty-year mortgage it can take as long as twenty-two years to pay off half the principal. This is because early in the life of a mortgage the majority of your payment goes to interest. You see, the interest you pay on a monthly basis is directly proportionate to the amount of principal you owe. Thus, as your monthly payments reduce your principal, the percentage of interest you pay on a monthly basis is reduced as well. The net effect is that the closer you get to the end of your loan term, the more principal debt you pay off.

Price appreciation provides the second way to build equity. Like the cost of other consumer products, home prices tend to go up over time. A cup of coffee doesn't cost a nickel anymore, and the home that Wini and Stanley bought for $8,000 in 1948 is worth a whole lot more these days. Historically, home prices have increased faster than the rate of inflation—over the past thirty years, inflation averaged 2 to 3 percent a year, while home prices went up on average 4 to 5 percent. This is a good fact to bear in mind if you ever find yourself in a market that doesn't currently appear to be experiencing appreciation. Given time, when you sell your home, we believe there can be an opportunity for you to experience both the bittersweet feeling of moving on and the excitement of making some money on the sale.

To be candid, when planned properly, your home can become a lot like an interest-bearing savings account. You make regular deposits with each mortgage check you write. Meanwhile, you have the opportunity to earn "bonus interest" through price appreciation on the value of your home over time. For that reason alone, home owners have a far greater net worth than renters.

It amazes most people to realize how much a 4 to 5 percent annual appreciation can amount to in thirty years. Figure 1.2 shows how a $150,000 home bought today would, at 4 percent annual appreciation, grow in value to $486,000 thirty years later. This may be hard to imagine until we realize that Stanley and Wini would never have believed in 1948 that their $8,000 home would ever be worth in the neighborhood of $400,000. And while appreciation absolutely varies from area to area and from time period to time period, over the long-term real estate appreciation is a proven and indisputable fact.

AS YOUR HOME APPRECIATES, YOUR EQUITY GROWS

Equity = Purchase Price + Appreciation − Remaining Debt

	$135,000 DEBT		$75,000 DEBT			
	$15,000 EQUITY		$280,000 EQUITY		$486,000 EQUITY	

CLOSING DAY		YEAR 22		YEAR 30	
Purchase price:	$150,000	Purchase price:	$150,000	Purchase price:	$150,000
Appreciation:	+ $0	Appreciation:	+ $205,000	Appreciation:	+ $336,000
Current home value:	$150,000	Current home value:	$355,000	Current home value:	$486,000
Remaining debt:	− $135,000	Remaining debt:	− $75,000	Remaining debt:	− $0
Total Equity =	**$15,000**	**Total Equity =**	**$280,000**	**Total Equity =**	**$486,000**

Simply put, equity is your home's value, minus the amount you still owe. Over time, your home's value can grow through appreciation. In the example above, you actually see how much it would grow with the historical appreciation of approximately 4 percent a year in the United States and Canada.

FIGURE 1.2

Figure 1.2 also shows the combined advantage of equity buildup and debt pay down. When you look at the home Sheila bought for $150,000 with only $15,000 down, you can see what happens in a dramatic way. After twenty-two years her $15,000 investment has turned into $280,000; and after thirty years (with her mortgage loan fully paid) it has grown to $486,000. By comparison, if she had put that $15,000 in the bank at 4 percent, it would be worth only $48,651 after thirty years. Amazingly, that's just one-tenth of what she gained through buying her home.

In addition to the two benefits of building equity through mortgage payments and appreciation, there's a third reason why buying a home is financially smart. The U.S. government allows a tax deduction for the interest paid on mortgage loans. We believe the significance of this deduction cannot be overlooked, especially in the first years of a mortgage, when interest makes up the bulk of your monthly payments. For example, if your loan payment was exactly the same as your rent, your annual housing costs, including property taxes and insurance, could actually be comparable once you factored in these mortgage interest tax savings. While tax deductions for interest paid are not the same in Canada, home owners do benefit from not having to pay a capital gains tax when they sell their primary residence.

There's another way to look at the buying vs. renting argument, using the example in Figure 1.3: if Sheila has a fixed-rate mortgage at 6 percent for thirty years and her property now is worth $150,000, over the life of her loan she would pay $324,000 in mortgage and interest payments. By comparison, Chris, over that same thirty years, would have paid more than $637,000 in rent assuming his monthly payment increased an average of 5 percent per year, the U.S. national average for the past thirty years. (If his landlord improbably never raised his rent for thirty years, he'd still pay more than $288,000.) But, at 4 percent annually, Sheila's home would have appreciated to more than $486,000, creating a positive equity gain of $162,000 ($486,000 less $324,000 in mortgage and interest payments). The bottom line after thirty years? Chris would have spent almost two-thirds of a million dollars, and Sheila would be free and clear on a home worth about half a million dollars.

CAN YOU REALLY AFFORD TO KEEP RENTING?

BUYING VS. RENTING

Sheila's $900 mortgage includes $700 of interest. Her total house payments are $10,800 annually. At the end of the year, $8,400 (12 months x $700) is tax deductible in the United States. She is in the 28 percent tax bracket, so her savings are $2,352. Her actual housing costs for the year are $8,448.($10,800 – $2,352).

Sheila's friend Chris believes he "can't afford" to buy. He pays $800 in rent each month.Chris's housing costs for the year are $9,600. So, even though he thinks he's saving money by renting, he actually spends about $1,150 more than Sheila – and he's not building any equity.

FIGURE 1.3

"I knew if I could afford to rent, I could afford to buy," says Donna Corbin, a twenty-one-year-old student in Las Vegas, Nevada, who bought her first home with a government-insured, no-down payment program. In other words, people who think they can't afford to buy might want to ask themselves a different question: "Can I really afford to keep renting?"

YOU DON'T HAVE TO KNOW EVERYTHING

You probably never realized you were surrounded by so many real estate "experts" until you decided to buy a home. All of a sudden, your coworker is telling you why fixed-rate loans are the only way to go, your great-aunt Martha in Palm Beach, Florida, is sharing her secret tips for finding a hot deal, and your father-in-law is e-mailing you postings from the real estate section of the Hometown Chronicle. Meanwhile, your Internet search engine is bringing up 2,342,209 Web pages, your boss is explaining why you should never buy north of the river, your hairdresser is urging you to never buy south of the river, and you're about ready to jump in the river.

Relax. Even if you can't stop the deluge of contradictory advice and divergent opinions, you don't have to let it stress you out. As an alternative, we offer you our biggest, most important, potentially most surprising rule for keeping your home-buying stress to a minimum—*you don't have to know everything*.

Keeping things simple starts with separating the things you need to know from those that are strictly optional. The home-buying knowledge you need falls into three categories: knowledge of the home-buying process itself, knowledge of your local market, and knowledge of your own personal criteria. Of those three, the only one you absolutely need to master is the last—what you want, what you need, and what you can afford. You need this knowledge to develop a clear vision of the home you're looking for. From there, your real estate agent will help you narrow the market to only those homes that fit your needs. Once you find that special property, the agent will also lead the way as your home is researched, assessed, negotiated, contracted, inspected, appraised, surveyed, fixed, financed, insured, and, finally, purchased.

Don't Let Fear Keep You From Making Your Smartest Investment

No one understands that "you don't have to know everything" better than Dawn Vaughn, an advertising account supervisor in Atlanta, Georgia. She delayed buying a home for years because she thought it would require tackling mountains of information. "You always hear these horror stories about home buying—that it's so difficult and there's so much you have to learn," she says.

However, once she made the jump, she was shocked by how easy the process became. "I remember leaving the closing table and thinking, 'That was so easy!'" she says. "I spent the next couple of months waiting for the phone to ring and for someone to tell us we owed a lot more money because we did it wrong."

Of course, the phone never rang because Dawn did it exactly right. "We found a great agent and a great mortgage broker who led us through the process and who we trusted to have our best interests in mind," says Dawn. "It made it so much easier not to have to know every little thing."

Of course, if you want to delve into the details, by all means, go ahead. We simply encourage you to remember that it's not necessary. It's perfectly reasonable to do what Dawn did—that is, to build a team you trust to handle the fuss.

THE FOUR FUNDAMENTAL PRINCIPLES OF THE REAL ESTATE BUYING PROCESS

No matter how much or how little you decide to learn about the details of your transaction, we've found four principles that apply to nearly any aspect of the process. In our years of experience, we have also identified some basic mistakes first-time home buyers are prone to make. Applying these proven principles will help you navigate through them.

Principle 1: The Rules of Real Estate Are Always Local

Markets change from year to year and from neighborhood to neighborhood. If you're shopping for a $150,000 home in San Antonio, Texas, you don't need any advice based on what the market was like when your parents bought, or what the market is like in Detroit, Michigan, or in fact, in the $300,000 neighborhood across the river in Windsor, Ontario. As for your brother-in-law's hot advice for scoring a Bay Area bungalow? Let it go. Your cousin's rules of real estate? Plug your ears. Or at the very least, take them with a great big grain of salt. You only need to understand what is available for $150,000 in San Antonio right now—nothing more, nothing less.

Similarly, we also encourage skepticism toward the simplistic advice you may have heard. You know what we mean: *Always offer below list price. Never look above your price range.* Adages and absolutes like these can blind you to the realities of your unique market, a specific property, or your personal needs and can keep you from seizing the opportunities before you.

Also, real estate laws, procedures, and practices are local. They vary significantly from province to province, state to state, and city to city. The way a real estate transaction closing was handled for your brother-in-law in California or your sister in Quebec may not be the way it's handled where you're buying your home. One of the key things your real estate agent will do for you is educate you on how real estate transactions are handled in your area and guide you step by step through the process.

Principle 2: The Best Deals Are Usually Win-Win

Everything in real estate is negotiable, so don't be afraid to ask for what you really want. Still, negotiations end when the parties involved become inflexible. The solution? Find a win-win outcome that accomplishes what both parties really need. That's why it's important to prepare for any real estate negotiation by deciding where you will and won't be willing to compromise. In the end, there is always a certain amount of give and take. You hold on to those things you really want, and you offer up those things that the other person wants and aren't as important to you. In chapter 5, we will show you how to craft a competitive offer in which both the buyer's priorities and the seller's needs are met. Remember, where there's a will, there's a way—a way to a great deal for you.

Principle 3: Price and Value Are Not the Same

A common mistake occurs when people focus on price, not value. This applies to the home you buy as well as the professionals you use. Being cost conscious is always wise but being value conscious is even wiser. Price and value normally correlate: you usually get what you pay for. But when looking beyond the surface, always be clear about what you want and what matters, and then expect to pay a fair price for these. Just because it's cheap doesn't make it a bargain. Think of buying a home as a search for value.

We also want you to think of value as quality at a reasonable price. Just as you seek out value in the home that you buy, also look for value from the professionals you hire. After all, you're more than likely making one of the biggest purchases of your life. This is no time to cut corners. That half-price inspector may save you $200 today but could miss a structural problem that costs you thousands tomorrow. You should be able to count on your lender to lock in the best rate and deliver all necessary paperwork by closing. If a discount lender drops the ball, your closing could be delayed, it could cost you considerably more money, or it might possibly even cause you to lose the home.

So don't set yourself up for hassles, headaches, or dead deals. Look for value—that is, integrity, reliability, and impeccable service—from all the professionals you hire. This principle has always been true and will always be true: you get what you pay for.

Principle 4: Choose With Your Heart and Your Head

Whatever property you buy will be both your home and a major financial investment. You want to find a home you absolutely love. A home that seems to fit your life located in a neighborhood that just feels right. At the same time, you want the property to be a solid financial asset—one that is structurally sound and appears to be well positioned to appreciate in the future. In the end, finding that perfect place for you means balancing emotion and rationality. When you're out looking for your future home, go ahead, let your heart guide you. But when it's time to buy, step back and think with a cool head. In a few years, when you may want to sell the house, you will be very glad you did.

THE EIGHT STEPS TO BUYING YOUR FIRST HOME

As you step out to buy your first home, a lot is going to happen. We want you to remember that you will be expertly guided through this process and, because of this, it will be easier than you think. However, a general understanding of each step along the way will make you more comfortable and confident. Each chapter of this book will introduce you to the language, concepts, and events you can expect as you move through the eight steps.

Congratulations! You've already taken the first step—you've decided to buy your first home. The next step is to find trusted advisers to guide you through the process. In chapter 2, we'll discuss how to choose a real estate agent who will educate you about your local market, negotiate on your behalf, and make sure no critical detail falls through the cracks.

> **The Eight Steps to Buying Your First Home**
>
> 1. Decide to buy.
> 2. Hire your agent.
> 3. Secure financing.
> 4. Find your home.
> 5. Make an offer.
> 6. Perform due diligence.
> 7. Close.
> 8. Protect your investment.

One of the first questions any buyer asks: what can I afford? This is definitely something to answer as soon as possible, and certainly before you fall in love with a home that ends up outside of your price range. The only way to know for sure is to get preapproved for a loan. Chapter 3 explains the factors you should consider as you weigh the many financing options available in today's mortgage market.

One of the most important things you must explore is your wants and needs to gain a clear understanding of what's most important in your future home—that is, you must develop your home-search criteria. Chapter 4 will prepare you for the kinds of questions to ask yourself during this critical stage. Armed with your home-search criteria and a preapproval letter, you'll be ready to go find the right home for you, and we'll equip you with proven strategies for your home search.

Chapter 5 will explain offer-writing and negotiating strategies that will make that home yours. However, the game doesn't end when the seller accepts your offer. The period from "contract to close" is when you and your lender make all necessary verifications (due diligence) to assure your home is financially, legally, and structurally sound. Chapter 6 will provide an overview of inspecting the property, making repairs, and reaching a final agreement with the sellers. Chapter 7 covers what to expect at the closing, and what can be done to make sure your closing is as smooth as possible. Finally, chapter 8 outlines our tips for taking good care of your home and increasing its value—as a place to live and as an asset to sell.

It may feel like an eternity from now, but some day in the not too distant future all the decisions will have been made. All your questions will have been answered. All the arrangements will have been prepared, checked, and double-checked. You'll sign the official papers on closing day, and your life as a home owner will actually begin!

THERE'S NO PLACE LIKE YOUR HOME

In short, finding a home isn't quite as easy as clicking your heels three times, but it doesn't have to resemble a battle with wicked witches and flying monkeys, either. With a trusted team of advisers and a handful of clear strategies, you'll have the knowledge and confidence to find the home that's right for you. And then, some day soon, you'll be there. You'll unpack the boxes, pick out draperies, toy with furniture arrangements, and send photos to friends. You'll feel that same satisfaction and excitement that Wini and Stanley felt in Levittown: *there really is no place like your home.*

Notes to Take Home

- Purchasing your own home is a great investment.
- Done right, home ownership lays the foundation for a life of financial security and personal choice.
- There are specific financial reasons to buy a home; among these are equity buildup, value appreciation, and tax benefits.
- Those who have the most fulfilling lives base their decisions on facts, not fears.
- The following facts help dispel fears about purchasing your first home:
    1. If you are paying rent, you very likely can afford to buy
    2. There is never a wrong time to buy the right home. All you need to do in the short run is find a good buy and make sure you have the financial ability to hold it for the long run
    3. The lack of a substantial down payment doesn't prevent you from making your first home purchase
    4. A less-than-perfect credit score won't necessarily stop you from buying a home
    5. The best way to get closer to buying your ultimate dream home is to buy your first home now
    6. Buying a home doesn't have to be complicated—there are many professionals who will help you along the way
- Here's the most important rule for keeping your stress to a minimum: you don't have to know everything.

MO'S FIRST HOME

     Growing up the daughter of a tenant farmer in Enid, Oklahoma, I always dreamed of owning my own home. My husband and I were thirty years old with two small children and living in a rental house in nearby Ponca City when God finally answered our prayers. We had saved a small amount of money for a down payment and put together a wish list. Then we learned that our neighbors who lived two doors down were planning to sell their house.

The house had everything we wanted: three bedrooms, two baths, and a nice-sized backyard for the children. It also had two big selling points—a large master bedroom that had been added and a huge family room with a fireplace and hearth. That big room is what sold us! I could see our families gathering around that big fireplace during holidays—our parents and siblings, nieces and nephews. All that, and it was in our price range—less than $20,000.

Excitedly, we approached our neighbors about buying their house. We purchased without the guidance of an agent, and our neighbors sold to us without an agent so they could save the cost of the commission. In retrospect, the transaction was not the easiest, but I still remember the thrill of finally having a home of our own and no longer being a renter.

Soon after we moved in, it started raining after a long drought. The house leaked like a sieve! We had to put buckets everywhere to keep from getting soaked. What a difficult turn of events for a young couple with two children and very limited finances. We had to use the money we had set aside to buy furniture so we could fix the roof instead. So, while our neighbors had saved a little money, we learned an important, costly lesson. From then on, we always used an agent.

Although we got off to a rocky start, I have wonderful memories of our first home. Raising our children. Visiting with our great neighbors. Watching our kids run in and out of the house and play in our backyard. All those dreams I had of sharing Thanksgiving and Christmas gatherings with the people we loved most sitting around that wonderful fireplace in our family room came true. It was even better than I had imagined.

We sold that house twelve years later for about $28,000 and put our equity into a brand-new home with 2,800 square feet. It felt like we had moved into a mansion. We still own that second home and stay there whenever we go back to Ponca City from Austin, Texas, where we live.

Our first little house taught us a lot. I learned that owning a home is a big responsibility. You have to keep up your house and lawn even when you don't have much money because that's part of being a good neighbor.

One of the biggest lessons I learned was not to let fear influence your decisions. When we bought our first home, we also had the option of buying a new one for just over $5,000 more. As a financially strapped young family, that amount scared us to death—even though we qualified to purchase it. That house sold for $50,000—around the same time we sold ours. The owners doubled their investment!

Most of all, I learned the joys of home ownership. As a tenant farmer's daughter, I probably appreciated it more than most people. After all this time, and all the houses we have owned, I still do.

Mo Anderson is vice chairman of the board of Keller Williams Realty, Inc.

CHAPTER 2:
HIRE YOUR AGENT

· · · · ·

In the beginning, acquiring real estate was simple. You went out, and you took it. In fact, that's how King William came to own all of England in 1066: he conquered it, declared it his own, and voilá, his it was. Of course, this was not a fair state of affairs for the vast majority of people involved. So over the years in many parts of the world, a fairer system developed where willing parties bought and sold their property. Take the 1803 Louisiana Purchase, in which France sold the middle third of North America to the United States. France wanted to sell, the United States wanted to buy, and the result was what has often been called the largest real estate deal in history. A 600-million-acre wedge of land stretching from Louisiana to Minnesota to Montana cost the young republic $15 million, which the government funded with a fifteen-year loan from a British bank at 6 percent interest.

Within the United States, the real estate revolution continued with the 1862 Homestead Act, which gave free land to anyone, including single women and freed slaves, who would farm the land. Settlers swarmed the West to stake their claims. Well into the nineteenth century, finding a home continued to be something people did for themselves. Some loaded up the wagon and found vacant bits of land in the West. (In Alaska, in fact, homestead land was available as late as 1986.) In cities, most buyers found property through personal or business networks and negotiated payment themselves.

THE REAL ESTATE AGENT: A PROFESSION IS BORN

By the late 1800s, though, cities had grown so big, people had claimed so much of the land, and the transactions had become much more complicated that specialists emerged who could keep close tabs on who was buying or selling, and who knew the ins and outs of brokering a transaction. The real estate profession was born. In 1908, real estate professionals from around the United States convened in Chicago to form the National Association of Realtors® (NAR). The group soon began laying the groundwork for the modern way real estate buyers and sellers in America would do business together—standardized contracts, open and clear procedures, accurate and timely property information, and perhaps most importantly, real estate licensing requirements and a code of ethics. From win-lose chaos to win-win order—the real estate industry progressed. About the same time all this was going on in the United States, a similar development occurred in Canada. In the 1880s, specialists on the west coast set up the first Real Estate Board in Vancouver. Later, real estate professionals established Boards throughout the country to address business ethics, industry standards, and to encourage a spirit of professional cooperation. From Vancouver to Calgary to Toronto, organized efforts across the nation culminated in the formation of CAREB, the Canadian Association of Real Estate Boards. CAREB soon implemented the "REALTOR" designation for its members, and eventually, The Canadian Real Estate Association (CREA) was formalized with its headquarters in Ottawa.

On one hand, the path to acquiring real estate has clearly evolved and become very straightforward. And, yet, at the same time, the process has unfortunately become more complex. In order to provide as much protection as possible for both buyer and seller, the legal, financing, and regulatory aspects of real estate transactions have become considerably more involved. From the required contractual disclosures and addendums to the procedures for determining clear title to property to the federally enforced regulations (such as Fair Housing, the Americans with Disabilities Act, and Truth in Lending), buyers, sellers, and the professionals who work with them are being held to ever higher standards.

> **A Buyer's Agent:**
> 1. Educates you about your market
> 2. Analyzes your wants and needs
> 3. Guides you to homes that fit your criteria
> 4. Coordinates the work of other needed professionals
> 5. Negotiates on your behalf
> 6. Checks and double-checks paperwork and deadlines
> 7. Solves any problems that may arise

So, although the straightforward path might lure some consumers into thinking they can do it themselves, the complexity of the process can trip them up. Unfortunately, they may not experience the trip-up until it's too late—they are so deeply into the contractual commitments of the transaction there is no easy way to recover. These people are often surprised by how many other issues and people impact their single transaction.

In fact, to give you an even clearer sense of how complicated things can get, Tulsa, Oklahoma, real estate agent Sherry Lewis once counted thirty-seven separate people involved in the typical real estate transaction in her area—insurance assessors, mortgage brokers and underwriters, inspectors, appraisers, escrow officers, buyer's agents, seller's agents, bankers, title researchers, and a couple of dozen other individuals whose actions and decisions have to be orchestrated in order to perform in harmony and get a home sale closed.

Who is the head coach of this complicated process with all these other players? That is the role of the licensed, professional real estate agent—the advocate for you and your interests throughout. It's much more than just finding the right home. The responsibilities your real estate agent must undertake before and after the home-showing phase are what makes having a real estate agent so invaluable. There are, we believe, seven distinct and critical roles your agent will play.

THE SEVEN MAIN ROLES OF YOUR REAL ESTATE AGENT

First and foremost, your agent will serve as your market consultant. That is, you will depend on your agent to educate you about your local real estate market and make sure you understand everything you need and want to know about the local home-buying process. We recommend you look for an agent who listens and then clearly communicates information in a way that makes sense to you. After orienting you to your market, your agent will help you analyze what exactly you need and want in a home—including things you may never have considered—so that when you take to the streets looking for homes, you'll know exactly what you're looking for. Then your agent will guide that home-to-home search for a property that meets all your needs and as many of your wants as possible.

"For most first-time home buyers, the process is overcast by fear of the unknown," says Canadian agent Rick Brash of Calgary, Alberta. He notes that many of his clients who haven't purchased a home before aren't sure what to do or where to go. "It's a huge gray area for them," Rick says, "and my job is to educate my clients about the market and make the process as enjoyable, efficient, and happy an experience as possible. I want my clients to have the time of their lives. That's my goal."

Your agent isn't the only expert whose assistance you'll need throughout the home-buying process. As you move ahead, other specialized advisers, such as a mortgage officer and property inspector, will also help you complete your purchase. Look for an agent who can expertly coordinate all the professionals involved in your home purchase.

Good Listening Skills Make All the Difference

When Mark and Toni Tolerico of the Bronx, New York, decided to buy their first home, they were more than ready. They had been married three years, were in their mid-twenties, were tired of living in a cramped apartment, and wanted a home in Lake Carmel, New York. They selected an agent who expertly guided them into their first home.

This agent carefully listened to Mark and Toni's wants and needs, and that same day she called back to say she had the perfect home for them to see. "We were your typical first-time home buyers who literally walked into the front door, and our knees started shaking because we knew it was the home we wanted," explains Toni. The Tolericos made an offer on the home that evening. "It was perfect," says Toni, "so perfect that we lived in that home for seventeen years."

Your agent's role as negotiator kicks in from the moment you make an offer on a home, and it doesn't stop until you've taken ownership and everything is settled. As a skilled negotiator, your agent will always represent your interests and push hard for the best deal without pushing so hard the deal is killed. If things do get tense, your agent will serve as a buffer between you and the seller or the seller's agent, remaining cool headed and logical while exploring different options to find the win-win. More often than you would think, your agent will actually continue to advocate for you well beyond the closing of the home due to unforeseen problems that can occur after you've taken ownership.

Throughout the closing process, a myriad of details will be resolved behind the scenes. Your agent will constantly check to see that time lines are met, paperwork is completed, updates have been filed, and the important steps are completed. Almost without fail, there will be problems. Your agent will prevent them when they can be anticipated and solve them when they are unforeseen. "Make sure you find an agent you feel comfortable with and can be completely honest with," says first-time home buyer Rondell Bennett of Fayetteville, North Carolina. "My husband and I felt completely at ease with our agent, Sherinne Anderson, and she made sure we received everything we needed."

In short, your real estate agent will wear many hats. You may find your agent through a strong referral from a trusted friend, relative, or colleague, or by your own research. No matter how you first meet your agent, we think it will benefit you both if you ask a few important questions. See examples on page 36.

PROFESSIONALISM: THE QUALITY THAT MATTERS ABOVE ALL ELSE

Trust and security in the hands of the right service provider are well placed, and for you, well deserved. The right real estate agent for you understands this and sees service as both a promise to you and a duty to the profession. The right agent for you will put your interests first, not just because it's a professional duty, but also because it is the right way to treat people. And cordiality is also good business. Successful agents enjoy the long-term benefits of providing stellar service and then being appreciated through testimonials and word-of-mouth referrals.

"Eighty-one percent of my business is repeat or referrals," says Gary Gentry, a long-time agent in Austin, Texas. "When you have satisfied clients, they want to continue to do business with you because they know you, like you, and trust you."

Good Agents Put Their Clients First, Their Paychecks Second

Phoenix, Arizona, agent Elaine Sans Souci once worked with a buyer who had been disabled by an accident. It severely limited the woman's memory, and she survived on a disability payment that barely covered her monthly costs.

"She was in the sort of situation where she could do laundry once a month, because she had exactly one dollar and twenty-five cents budgeted for laundry,"

Elaine explained. "When I met her, the mortgage company said, 'Run.'"

But Elaine didn't run. She spent months helping the client get her finances in shape and looking for a home that would save her money. Finally, when she got a property under contract, the client suddenly remembered some recurring costs she had forgotten to tell her lender. With that new information, Elaine realized that there was no way the woman would be able to keep up with the payments. She convinced her client to drop out of the deal.

"Sure, it's hard to walk away from a commission," she says. "But you can't just watch a client get into a situation where you know she'll go down the tubes."

But this story has a good ending: Elaine eventually found a home her client could afford.

KNOW WHAT TO EXPECT

We've all experienced situations where we felt like someone wasn't really listening to what we were saying. You can probably think of one right now—a time when you talked with a salesperson in a store or called your bank or telephone company service representative, and the person didn't get what you were asking. In fact, the representative didn't seem to be listening, and service fell far short of your expectations. Research shows that as consumers we value those professionals who listen carefully and are able to meet or exceed our expectations.

Scott and Lori Dumon of Jacksonville, Florida, bought their first home in Roswell, Georgia. "We were really excited—and nervous. Our out-of-state wedding was less than a month away, and we still had a million things to do, but buying the home early would give us time to get the home ready before we moved in," Lori recalls.

"Our real estate agent was thorough. She helped us get preapproved for a mortgage before we started previewing property, explained every step of the process, and gave us the reassurance we needed at a time when our schedules were crazy."

Their agent thoroughly researched neighborhoods and properties. "She narrowed down the choices to save us as much time and stress as possible," Scott says.

When you have an agent who truly listens to you, you will also want to listen back. You will be told exactly what you can expect and what will happen during the home-buying process. This is your opportunity to get very detailed about your mutual expectations—ask how often you'll be in contact, how often you can expect to see homes, and how many properties you might visit in an afternoon. Ask your agent how communications will be handled; by phone, fax, or e-mail, and make sure you share your preferences. Ask if there will be others helping your agent who may be contacting you so that you're not surprised when they do.

When you find the right agent, you will actually be making a mutual commitment. Your new agent will be dedicated to answering all your questions and getting you

---

Code of Ethics and Standards of Practice

NATIONAL ASSOCIATION OF REALTORS® (NAR)
Duties to Clients and Customers
Article 1 When representing a buyer, seller, landlord, tenant, or other client as an agent, REALTORS® pledge themselves to protect and promote the interests of their client. This obligation to the client is primary, but it does not relieve REALTORS® of their obligation to treat all parties honestly. When serving a buyer, seller, landlord, tenant or other party in a non-agency capacity, REALTORS® remain obligated to treat all parties honestly.

CANADIAN REAL ESTATE ASSOCIATION (CREA)
As REALTORS®, we accept a personal obligation to the public and to our profession. The Code of Ethics of the Canadian Real Estate Association embodies these obligations. As REALTORS®, we are committed to: Professional competent service; Absolute honesty and integrity in business dealings; Co-operation with and fairness to all; Personal accountability through compliance with CREA's Standards of Business Practice.

what you want. You will be committing to honestly sharing your feelings, opinions, and concerns. And you will be committing to work exclusively with that person as your agent. This is usually done formally through a Buyer Representation Agreement.

The Buyer Representation Agreement

Any strong relationship is built on respect for each party's needs, expectations, and time. That's why many agents like to set mutual expectations with a Buyer Representation Agreement. This document states that any home you buy, you will buy with the help of your agent for the duration of the agreement. Such agreements can usually be terminated with a couple of days' notice, although you usually can't terminate the agreement and then go buy a house that your agent showed you three days before.

A representation agreement can help you by giving your agent the confidence that the time devoted to your home search will not go unpaid. This in turn gives you the agent's very focused attention. These agreements are also useful because they spell out the precise duties you can expect your agent to fulfill, so if they are not, you can point to the agreement and request an explanation. It is actually a true win-win.

All in all, a Buyer Representation Agreement involves making a mutual written commitment that clarifies the working relationship.

In the end, we truly believe it's important to find the right real estate agent for you. Finding the right agent isn't complicated but will require effort and diligence on your part—it's simply the best way to get your home search off on the right foot. Knowing you've put in due diligence to find an agent you like and trust, it will help you feel more.

Notes to Take Home

- When looking for an agent, know that above all else good agents put their clients first.

- Your real estate agent will perform seven main roles:
    1. Educate you about your market.
    2. Analyze your wants and needs.
    3. Guide you to homes that fit your criteria.
    4. Coordinate the work of other needed professionals.
    5. Negotiate on your behalf.
    6. Check and double-check paperwork and deadlines.
    7. Solve any problems that may arise.

- The Buyer Representation Agreement clarifies the working relationship between the buyer and the real estate agent. It involves making a mutual written commitment—your agent commits to getting you what you want, and you commit to working exclusively with your agent.

DAVE'S FIRST HOME

When we moved to East Lansing, Michigan, my wife, Sherry Dawn, was pregnant with our first child. Twenty-seven months later we had three children—two of our own and a young girl we adopted. It was 1969, and my wife and I were living in a residence hall on the campus of Michigan State University while I worked toward a doctorate in counseling psychology. I was the residence hall director. Three young children and a hundred babysitters—what's not to like?

The students adored our kids, but there was no privacy for a young family, nor enough space. It was clear that there was no way we could live in a student residence hall with three children.

In looking for our first home, we were purely practical. My wife and I both were from rural areas in New York State and were familiar with simple country living. We needed a home we could afford. We found one—a small, two-bedroom, one-story house in an older neighborhood with lawns and trees—and bought it with a no-money-down Federal Housing Administration (FHA) loan. When we shut the door to our new home, we enjoyed complete privacy together for the first time in our lives.

It turned out to be a wonderful, cozy home for a beginning family. The house was probably twenty-five to thirty years old and needed some fixing up. I bought a Time-Life book on home remodeling and repair and enlisted a friend who knew something about wiring. We plunged in, building out the attic and adding two more bedrooms, among other improvements.

I knew that I was in way over my head. But it was a lot of fun rehabbing my own home and creating a room for each of our children with my own hands. As amateur as my work was, it was good enough. We purchased the house for around $30,000. Eighteen months later I took a full-time job at my alma mater in Albany, New York, and we sold it for a profit.

I learned so much from that experience. My adolescence had been extended because as a college student and staff member I had spent years living in fraternity houses and dormitories on several campuses. Buying that home was my first step to serious adulthood. Looking back I see now that the home was very much like the one I grew up in—down to the refinished walk-in attic.

I believe, in a way, I was following in my dad's footsteps—buying a house and, through my own labor, making it into a home for my family that we could be proud of. We loved our time there—eating dinner together, playing catch on the lawn, and visiting with neighbors. I finally felt like a dad and a grown-up.

Even though necessity drove me to it, I learned that owning a home was a smart thing to do. I remember I was considering a rental, but my real estate agent really encouraged me to buy instead. He was right. I used the money I made from the sale to buy our next home, an even better one. I saw right away that home ownership was a good economic move. Ten years later I joined the real estate business. That very first home was partly responsible for starting me on this fulfilling path.

Coauthor Dave Jenks served as vice president of research and development at Keller Williams Realty International from 1996 to 2008.

CHAPTER 3:
SECURE FINANCING

· · · · ·

Teresa Van Horn of Madison, Wisconsin, never thought she'd qualify for a mortgage. After getting married at an early age to a financially challenged individual, as she referred to him, she found herself broke, divorced, and drowning in debt, all before her twenty-fifth birthday. Although she was able to move in with her parents and sort things out, she did pay some bills late and came close to defaulting on her student loans more than once. She thought her credit was ruined forever.

Less than five years later, Teresa had a steady job and a stable income and was regularly paying off her debts. She was ready to stop renting, but one obstacle stood in the way: facing her credit report. "It took a long time for me to get up the guts to talk to lenders," she says. "I thought they would laugh at me."

They didn't—in fact, Teresa was pleasantly surprised to learn she qualified for a modest loan.

While you may find the thought of home ownership thrilling, the thought of taking on a mortgage may be downright chilling. Many first-time buyers, like Teresa, start out confused about the process or nervous about making such a large financial commitment. A mortgage is a serious responsibility and warrants very careful attention to what you can truly afford and what kind of mortgage can best help you reach your financial goals. However, a mortgage is also a tremendous privilege. Imagine: if you couldn't borrow the money to buy your home, you'd have to pay cash. If you thought coming up with a down payment was challenging, imagine what it would be like to save the whole purchase price! "In India, you usually have to pay cash up front, so families save their whole lives just to buy a house," says Dita Niyogi, who bought her first home in Texas with a mortgage.

In general, you'll probably discover that mortgage loans are less confusing than you might imagine. Actually, what appears as a vast array of loan choices in the mortgage market today are all just simple variations on a few major types. Once you understand the basic elements of a mortgage, which this chapter clearly and simply explains, you'll be much better prepared to choose the best one for you.

MORTGAGE 101

What exactly is a mortgage loan? In its most basic sense, a mortgage loan is the borrowing of money (loan) secured by a real estate property (mortgage). As a buyer, you can obtain your mortgage loan from a mortgage banker, mortgage broker, savings and loan, credit union, or bank. Beyond the traditional mortgage industry, you may be able to obtain some or all of the financing from private individuals, even in some cases the seller of the property. Funding from these private sources is often called "creative financing," which we cover later in this chapter.

Contrary to what some people believe, lenders dread the thought of foreclosure—the process of seizing a home from someone who isn't making their payments. When lenders have to foreclose, they lose interest revenue and face the costs and hassle of getting the property resold. In short, we want you to recognize that reputable lenders are in the money-lending business, not the home ownership business, and so they don't want you to take on a monthly payment beyond what you can afford.

6 Steps to Financing a Home

1. Choose a loan officer (or mortgage specialist).
2. Make a loan application and get approved.
3. Determine what you want to pay and select a loan option.
4. Submit to the lender an accepted purchase offer contract.
5. Get an appraisal and title commitment.
6. Obtain funding at closing.

To make sure you don't get in over your head, lending institutions carefully analyze your finances to come up with an estimate of what you can afford. To start this process, you submit an application to a loan officer (or to a mortgage specialist as they are also commonly referred to) detailing your income, assets, and debts. The loan officer will help you explore your financing options and figure out roughly how much you can borrow and the kind of loan that will work best for you. "I look at a buyer's gross income, monthly debt, and credit score. Once I have that information, I can assess what loan programs the buyer will qualify for and which of these programs have the lowest rates," says Dawn Skinner, a loan officer in Austin, Texas.

Once you have a general game plan, your application goes to an underwriter who makes sure all the information checks out, and then decides exactly how much the institution is willing to lend you. This whole process is called preapproval; the application will take about an hour of your time, and underwriting usually takes a few days, but in some cases may take longer. Computerized underwriting has actually allowed for some applications to be completed and approved in a matter of hours, but it is generally wise to expect it to take a bit longer. We consider preapproval paramount to your home-buying success, and we discuss it at several points in this chapter.

From start to finish, you will follow a six-step, easy-to-understand process to securing the financing for your first home.

A Conversation About Financing Your Home

To answer some common first-time home-buyer questions and help guide you through the financing aspects of the home-buying process, we'd like to share with you an informative conversation between a first-time home buyer and a real estate agent.

BUYER *I'm ready to start looking for a loan, but I'm not sure where to begin. Should I start by shopping rates?*

AGENT Actually, no. A common mistake many home buyers make is to start by shopping around for rates when they should really be shopping around for the best loan officer.

BUYER *Why is that?*

AGENT The advertised rates don't necessarily have any bearing on the rates you'll get. The rate you get will be most dependent on the loan program you choose. The right loan officer will put you into the best program for you. And honestly, rates for comparable programs can almost always be matched by many lenders—a great loan officer will put you in the right program and get you the best rate for it. Great loan officers always work with great lenders. When you find one, you'll find the other. And great lenders bring with them the expertise and integrity to process your application in a timely manner and deliver the rate you signed up for.

BUYER	*Sounds easy enough. So, how do I choose the right loan officer for me?*
AGENT	You begin by asking for a referral. Do you know anyone who has a good loan officer they've worked with in the past? If not, I can give you the names of several experienced loan officers my clients regularly work with. If a referral is not the route for you, I'd suggest you select three or four lenders and simply interview their loan officers. The key is to find the one loan officer and lender you feel is trustworthy and competent to handle your loan. Remember, a good loan officer will absolutely make all the difference in the world.
BUYER	*Should I look for a mortgage banker or a mortgage broker? What's the difference?*
AGENT	Both can lend you money for a home loan, but they are different. Mortgage bankers include banks, credit unions, and savings and loans. While they do provide in-house approval and an understanding of local market conditions, they almost always exclusively offer their own loan products, which can possibly mean less rate and program flexibility. The usual difference between the two types of lenders is that mortgage bankers originate the loans and do their own underwriting, while mortgage brokers typically do not. However, mortgage brokers generally offer more loan program options. Think of it this way: bankers lend you money from their bank; brokers shop your loan to many lenders.

BUYER	*Once I have a loan officer and lender, what's the next step?*
AGENT	Your loan officer will ask you to fill out an application, and you'll provide the details of your personal finances, such as source of income, information on your assets and debts, Social Security number, work history, and some additional financial details. The lender will then examine your credit and debt history and also look at your credit score, which is a big determinant of your mortgage worthiness.
BUYER	*That's quite a bit of information. What do lenders really want to know?*
AGENT	They basically want to know what you earn, what you owe, what funds you have available for down payment and how financially responsible you have been.
BUYER	*Will the loan application cost me anything?*
AGENT	You may be asked to pay a nominal fee for your credit report. You should ask your loan officer for a copy of your credit report as well. It never hurts to review it for errors.
BUYER	*Do I have to work only with that loan officer or lender?*
AGENT	Absolutely not. You're under no contract, so you can change at any time if you wish to explore your lending options elsewhere.

BUYER	*Great. That makes me feel better. What happens with the completed application?*
AGENT	The loan officer submits your application to the lender's underwriting department. The underwriter will review all your submitted information, such as your verified income, assets, debts, and so forth, and then approve you for a specified home loan amount.
BUYER	*Approved? Does that mean I'll be prequalified to go house hunting?*
AGENT	Great question. You really want to go beyond prequalification and seek preapproval. Preapproval is an actual letter of verification based on your finances that states you are preapproved for a loan at a certain amount. Prequalification is a best-guess estimate based on your profile, not a guarantee; preapproval is a firm commitment by your lender for a certain loan amount in writing. This is really important as you go out and look for a home, especially if you end up making an offer on a home that garners multiple offers. The preapproval letter is your ticket to making a more earnest offer on a home and that just might encourage the seller to work with you and your offer over the others. With this, the seller knows with certainty that you have the financing in place to buy the home.
BUYER	*So, if I'm preapproved for a certain amount, do I have to borrow the entire amount?*
AGENT	Not at all. You borrow the loan amount you need and are comfortable with. You may prefer to borrow less than the amount that you are preapproved for.

BUYER	*You mean I'll get preapproval for a certain loan amount, but I don't actually have to use the entire amount. That gives me some flexibility. But then what about the type of loan?*
AGENT	Your loan officer will give you options for the types of loans available, and there are several. For example, in the United States you may want a conventional thirty-year fixed-rate loan. Or, as a first-time buyer, you might qualify for a thirty-year fixed-rate government-sponsored loan if the loan amount is within the right range. You might even prefer an adjustable-rate mortgage (ARM), which is usually referred to as a variable-rate mortgage in Canada, or some variation of it. We'll ask your loan officer to walk you through each type and then consider what works best for you. (Since thirty-year fixed-rate loan programs are not available in Canada, buyers typically work with a mortgage specialist to select an amortization period, such as twenty-five years, and a term, or length of time, such as five years, in which they lock in a fixed rate. Speak with your mortgage specialist for details.)
BUYER	*Good, I'll have several types of loans to choose from. But who decides the amount I'll be paying each month?*
AGENT	The loan officer will work with you based on three factors: how much you want to spend as a down payment, your interest rate, and the term (that is the length) of your loan.

BUYER	*Down payment, rate, and term. I've got it. Let's start with the down payment—do I have to put a lot of money down then?*
AGENT	Not at all. A conventional mortgage can require as little as a 5 percent down payment, and there are even some programs out there that can help you put down less. In particular, there are government programs designed to help first-time buyers that allow you to minimize your down payment and get a favorable loan rate and term. If this interests you, we can ask your loan officer if you qualify for government-sponsored loan programs.
BUYER	*I'm fortunate I've saved enough for my down payment. But what if other expenses suddenly affected my down payment savings fund, and I no longer had enough money for a down payment?*
AGENT	We'd have to think creatively and look beyond your bank account and normal income. What assets do you have that you can sell to raise the money for your down payment? Does your family have an extra car or maybe a boat and trailer you don't really need? How about old furniture, appliances, clothes, and other belongings you can part with in a garage sale? Maybe you could sell some collectibles on eBay you no longer want? Or, perhaps you can ask relatives and friends for a cash gift. Since you are getting married soon, you could ask for cash instead of gifts on your wedding registry. Think outside the box, think without limits here, and see what ideas come up. Let me tell you about Gary Keller, the founder of Keller Williams Realty. He bought his first property for about $40,000 (many, many years

ago!), by somewhat unconventional means. He didn't have the savings for a down payment. What he did have was a nearly paid-off Honda Accord. So, to get the funds he needed, he decided to refinance his car and used the loan money as his down payment.

BUYER *I see what you're saying. There are actually many creative ways we could generate cash for a down payment, and if push came to shove I could even be happy to part with the clutter I no longer use. At this point, let's say I'm preapproved and have the down payment money. Now can I go looking for a home to buy?*

AGENT Absolutely. We're ready to go. Once you are certain about the home you want, you'll make an offer based on the amount you've been approved for. Let's say it has three bedrooms, a nice big bathroom, and the right kind of yard with the gardening possibilities you've envisioned. And then let's assume your offer is accepted. What you'll do next is submit that accepted contract to your lender on a specific property at a specific price. This will inform your lender as to exactly how much you actually need to borrow.

BUYER *I understand. The contract offer helps determine the amount I'll need to borrow. What's next?*

AGENT With your offer contract in place, the lender will provide you with a "good faith estimate" detailing the exact loan you can be offered as well as the fees and down payment you'll likely pay at closing. It's called a good faith estimate because it's the lender's best approximation of these charges. Some may vary slightly. If you've locked in your interest rate on the loan, that won't change. The next step is to get an appraisal on the home and make sure you will be able to receive a clear title.

BUYER   *What's an appraisal for and who does it?*

AGENT   Both of these are great questions. The appraisal verifies the value of the home for the lender. The lender will give you a loan based on the appraised value or sales price, whichever is less. Of course you would hope that the home appraises for at least what you offered to pay for it. An appraiser is the certified professional hired by your lender to make a fair market assessment of the value of your property (an appraisal) based on several factors, including location, condition, and comparable sales from the immediate area. The title company involved in the transaction will check to see if the property has clear title. (In Canada a real estate lawyer will verify if the property has clear title.)

BUYER   *Well, what exactly is clear title, anyway? I mean, this will be my home, right?*

AGENT   Yes, this will be your home—as long as the seller has a clear title to transfer to you. To make sure the title is clear and can be conveyed, a title company has to confirm if any liens or unpaid claims have been placed against the property. For example, a lien can be money owed for work performed by a contractor on the property that must be resolved or paid before the transfer of the property to you. A title company also assures you that the sellers are the true and only owners of the property and have the full rights to sell it to you. (In Canada a real estate lawyer fulfills these duties, and each province has its own government-directed Land Title Office to guarantee transfer of title.)

BUYER   *Ah, I see. In other words, if there are no liens or confused ownership, then we are clear to close, and the property becomes mine?*

AGENT   Yes, that's it. Upon closing, the final step, your lender immediately agrees to a transfer of funds to the seller, and you now own your first home. Now, there is one last thing you might want to know. Unlike rent, which is paid at the first of the month and then you live in the property, a mortgage is paid at the end of the month, after you've lived in your home. So, if you close before the end of the month, the lender will go ahead and collect the payment you'd owe for the days between closing and the end of the month, and then you won't owe another payment for an entire month. Now you can relax, knowing you don't have to make your first payment until up to thirty-one days from the date you closed.

BUYER   *This is now all very clear to me. Let's get moving then!*

AGENT   Onward!

We hope this buyer-agent discussion enlightened you on the basic steps of the home-financing process. And we encourage you to think about any questions you might have and write them down so you can address them later with your agent. In the meantime, keep the six steps listed on page 47 in mind and think about each step as an interdependent part of a logical process. The remainder of the chapter further explains steps 1 and 3. Since we've explained the loan application aspect of step 2 in the dialogue, we'll revisit loan preapproval later. We'll consider steps 4-6 in greater depth in subsequent chapters, since they occur after you've searched for and found the home you want to buy.

CHOOSING THE RIGHT LOAN OFFICER AND LENDER

Once you know your mortgage loan priorities, you'll be ready to talk to loan officers about the specific packages they offer. Loan officers can give you a ballpark estimate of the kinds of loans and interest rates you qualify for and the fees their lender charges. While it may be tempting to choose the loan officer and lender strictly based on the lowest quoted rate, we recommend prioritizing by a different standard—their reputation. Referrals from friends, your real estate agent, and other people you trust are the best way to find a reputable loan officer and lender who can get the job done. In the end, having the right loan officer working for you can assure that all the details will be handled in an accurate and timely manner and that the loan officers are giving you sound financial advice. Your peace of mind is paramount.

The process of finalizing a loan has many steps. Piles of paperwork have to be drawn up, verified, processed, and signed by multiple parties—all within a very short time frame. Mistakes can delay this process or even derail the transaction completely. As a result, nearly every real estate agent has at least one horror story, if not many, about buyers who chose a loan officer and lender based on a low-rate quote, only to find that once they reached the closing table the rate was higher than promised. Agent Elaine Sans Souci, for example, worked with a couple who chose an online lender over her objections. The couple could afford a monthly payment of no more than $900 and informed the online lender. The lender then sent a loan commitment letter that promised a $900 monthly payment but didn't explain that the $900 only included principal and interest. Based on this letter, the couple made an offer on an ideal property. However, when Elaine reviewed the full paperwork with the couple, she calculated that the couple's real monthly payment, including taxes and insurance, would actually be about $1,300. "There was no way they could afford the payments, so they lost the house," says Elaine.

On the other hand, we know great loan officers and their lender can work wonders. Agent Jennifer Barnes of Atlanta, Georgia, worked with a couple whose lender was simply missing in action on closing day. "When we got to the closing table, there was no one to be found," she says. "There was no loan package, no nothing." Jennifer snapped into action to get a new loan processed in less than a week, relying on her strong relationship with a lending team.

In short, an irresponsible loan officer or lender can ruin your purchase. So, keep yourself safe: start your loan search by shopping referrals, not shopping rates. Of course, rates and fees do matter. They matter a lot! The right loan officer will let you know ahead of time all of the rates and fees for their lender's loan products you are considering, so you will know if they are fair and competitive. In the end, the lender will provide you a good-faith estimate that details the loan officer's best forecast of what you qualify for, what interest rate you can get, and all the fees involved.

BE READY FOR CLOSING COSTS

Lender's fees and other closing costs in the United States
can add 3 to 5 percent to your home's purchase price.

LIKELY LENDER FEES

1. Origination fee ("points")
2. Administration fee
3. Application fee
4. Broker or lender fee
5. Commitment fee
6. Document preparation
7. Underwriting fee

LIKELY THIRD-PARTY FEES

1. Credit report
2. Home appraisal
3. Pest inspections
4. Recording fees
5. Settlement fees
6. Survey
7. Tax and insurance prepayment
8. Title search
9. Title insurance
10. Courier services

AND ALWAYS ASK

"What other costs will I be responsible for to get our home closed?"

What Difference Do Fees Make?

While fees are rarely associated with home loans in Canada, in the United
States they are commonplace. So, on closing day in the United States, you may
be responsible for various fees and expenses on top of your down payment.
Closing costs include the lender's own fees, third-party fees for requirements
such as title insurance, and the cost of prepaying a year's worth of property
insurance. Because closing costs can run in the thousands of dollars, it's a good
idea to compare what different lenders charge. Line-by-line comparisons can be

confusing, so instead, when you get your good-faith estimates, we suggest you compare the total costs. If Lender A is more expensive than Lender B, don't be afraid to ask why. Sometimes lenders will negotiate.

In the United States, one cost you should consider is "points," or prepaid interest. One point equals 1 percent of the total loan amount—one point on a $100,000 loan is $1,000.

In general, loans with higher (more) points come with lower interest rates. If you think about it, this makes perfect sense—when you pay more interest up front, the lender doesn't need to collect as much interest every month to make a profit. In high interest-rate environments, buyers sometimes pay extra points to buy a lower interest rate. However, this strategy pays off only over a longer period of time. For example, you wouldn't want to pay thousands up front to save $100 or so a month if you were going to move in a few years. So, if you're considering paying points, we suggest you ask your lender or agent to walk you through the math just to make sure it's worth the investment.

SHORT ON CASH? ASK THE SELLER TO PAY CLOSING COSTS

One way to minimize up-front expenses is to ask the seller to pay some or all of your closing costs.

Banker vs. Broker: Does It Matter?

Your list of recommended loan officers and lenders will likely include both mortgage bankers and mortgage brokers. Either can do a fine job of securing a mortgage for you, but it's helpful to understand the differences between them. And even though we covered this in our dialogue, we just want to make sure you're clear on the difference.

Mortgage bankers typically approve and then make their own loans, meaning their loan officers are intimately familiar with their company's mortgage products. This enables them to predict with great certainty what their underwriters will approve. In-house approval can also help solve problems if they emerge. "The whole company has a stake in getting that loan closed," explains Phoenix, Arizona, agent Steve Chader. On common products (such as a thirty-year fixed rate in the United States), we want to emphasize that different banks will usually offer almost the same rate, making it easy for you to choose based on reputation and referrals.

Mortgage brokers specialize in shopping the mortgage market to find the right loan for their clients with mortgage bankers. Because they typically deal with many mortgage bankers, brokers can offer a wider variety of mortgage products. However, since they aren't actually underwriting the loan, it may take longer to get approvals, and there may not be as much flexibility in the qualification process.

Whether you choose a mortgage banker or a mortgage broker, the next step is to fill out an application and get preapproved. Preapproval will let you know the most you can borrow—and when added to your down payment, it sets a ceiling for your price range. However, to really pinpoint your target home purchase price, don't simply rely on your lender's preapproval. We want you to talk it over with your real estate agent or your financial adviser. Lenders determine what you can borrow, but only you can decide what you can afford. First-time home buyer Jeffrey Barg in Philadelphia, Pennsylvania, decided to consult with a financial planner on how much he should invest in his home purchase. "Since I wasn't leaving Philadelphia anytime soon, buying a home made financial sense. My planner confirmed this and helped me figure out how much I could spend. I used that information as a guideline," says Jeffrey.

KNOW YOUR MORTGAGE OPTIONS

Mortgage loans now come in more varieties than ever. However, we want to point out that the differences among them boil down to three basic factors:

1. Down payment
2. Interest rate
3. Term

Special Loans for Special Needs

The mortgage industry has hundreds, if not thousands, of niche products to fit different buyers' unique situations. First-time buyers, for example, often qualify for local and federal programs to encourage home ownership, such as an FHA loan; low-income buyers and veterans also have special opportunities available to them.

Another option is an interest-only loan. These loans have lower monthly payments, so they're a tool for certain kinds of investors who only plan to hold onto a property for a short amount of time. Regardless of the loan you choose, as a first-time home buyer you should be wary of a mortgage situation with a temptingly low monthly payment: it will dramatically increase the total amount you pay for your home over time, delay equity buildup for years, and possibly place you in a difficult financial bind in the future if your payments increase dramatically, or if you are forced to sell quickly.

As a matter of principle when buying your first home, we strongly recommend buying a home you can afford without resorting to specialized loan products that simply work to reduce your initial monthly payments. We suggest you look into the benefits of time-tested mortgage opportunities such as an FHA loan and similar first-time home-buyer programs.

Down Payment

In the past, buying a home required a 20 percent down payment. Now, buyers can get into properties by putting a much lower percentage down. However, that 20 percent mark (which in lending-land is called "having an 80 percent loan-to-value ratio," or "80 percent LTV") has its advantages. For one thing, we believe it usually gets you the best interest rate. Plus, the more you put down, the less you have to borrow—that means a lower monthly payment, as well as paying less interest over the life of the loan. Putting 20 percent down also frees you from private mortgage insurance, "PMI" in the United States, which lenders require of buyers who borrow a higher percentage. In Canada, mortgage loan insurance is primarily provided through the government-sponsored Canada Mortgage and Housing Corporation (CMHC). In the United States, borrowers have to pay a monthly PMI fee, but in Canada a borrower's mortgage loan insurance is actually added to the principal loan amount.

PMI is good for lenders, as it protects them against loss if a borrower defaults on a low down-payment loan. PMI can also be good for you, the borrower with less cash, if paying PMI is the only way you can get a mortgage. However, know that it's basically just a lender protection fee that increases your monthly payment, and the PMI portion of your monthly payment is not tax-deductible. One important note: after a couple of years when your principal payments, combined with your down payment, reach that 20 percent mark, you are eligible to have the PMI policy canceled in the United States. Many home owners don't know this and continue to pay PMI needlessly; however, in the United States, some states require that the lender remove the PMI once the remaining loan balance is estimated to be below a certain loan-to-value (LTV). It is important to know that you may have to take the initiative to cancel PMI with your lender.

Now, over time, as your home increases in value (appreciation), the amount you have borrowed (principal) will steadily become a smaller and smaller percent of the home's actual worth. If you decide to refinance, the new lender will calculate your new loan amount against the new appraised value of your home. Therefore, your loan-to-value (LTV) ratio could now be at or below the 80 percent threshold, and you will not need to pay for PMI on this new loan.

Private Mortgage Insurance: Know Your Options

When Julie Stephen and her husband Tom, of Austin, Texas, bought their first home in 1991, they only had $10,000 to put down on an $80,000 home (which was a little less than 13 percent of the purchase price). So their lender accepted the $10,000 down payment and added PMI. The PMI payments ran about $35 a month. After being in the home for five years, with property taxes increasing every year, that $35 payment really began to irk Julie and Tom. So, they decided to refinance. Not only were interest rates lower, but they had also built up equity in the home. In fact, the home was then worth $110,000: the $68,000 they still owed was now only 62 percent of the current value of the home, so the lender no longer required them to have PMI. The final result? A lower monthly payment—without the PMI tacked on.

A common way to get around mortgage loan insurance from the start is to take out a second loan, which is often called a "piggyback" in the United States. This is a loan that covers the difference between the cash you have and the cash you need to hit that magical 20 percent mark. For example, if you have 5 percent to put down, you could take out an "80-15-5": an 80 percent first loan, a 15 percent second loan, and a 5 percent down payment. An 80-10-10 is another common variation, or you may even be able to find a second loan to cover the entire down payment. Typically, you'll pay a higher rate on this second loan, but they are usually for a shorter period of time. Importantly, because the second loan is a home loan instead of an insurance fee, in the United States the interest is tax-deductible. "I always recommend structuring a loan so that you don't have to pay PMI. You can take tax deductions on your interest payments and build equity more quickly," says loan officer Dawn Skinner.

Without a doubt, paying 20 percent down on a home is a sound financial decision. Having a large equity position in your home from day one protects you from unforeseen shifts in the real estate market and lays a solid financial foundation for your future. If you elect another option, we encourage you to consider making additional investments in your home—from making repairs or improvements that add value to simply accelerating your principal payments (making additional payments above your monthly mortgage amount).

Interest Rate

We realize everybody wants the lowest interest rate possible. In addition to the fact that a lower rate can save you thousands of dollars over the life of the loan, it will also reduce the amount you pay each month or allow you to buy a more expensive property with the same payment. The example in figure 3.1 shows that for a monthly payment of just under $1,000, on a 6 percent loan would allow you to buy a home that's worth $30,000 more than the home you could get with a loan at 8 percent.

Sometimes people put off buying a home thinking that the market or interest rate will go down. We would encourage you to move forward with the purchase of your first home because you may find the rates will rise rather than drop and that "golden" opportunity you were waiting for may pass you by.

The typical scenario: a home buyer will read in the newspaper that interest rates are expected to fall. "CENTRAL BANK SET TO DROP RATES!" is the classic headline. What mortgage brokers understand, and what we think you need to understand, is that today's mortgage rates almost always reflect these changes before they happen. When the U.S. Federal Reserve or Canada's Central Bank lowers the prime lending rates, most mortgage rates will already reflect that anticipated change as a function of the highly competitive world of trying to win your mortgage business. So while these buyers think they are smartly timing the market, they may be waiting for a rate drop that won't happen or that already has, and in the meantime, they may see their dream home go up in price.

INTEREST RATES IMPACT HOW MUCH HOUSE YOU CAN AFFORD

If you can afford a $1,000 monthly mortgage payment (not including taxes and insurance), a low interest rate can allow you to afford a higher-priced home. Your rate will also determine how much interest you pay over the life of your loan.

LOAN AMOUNT	INTEREST RATE	MONTHLY P&I PAYMENT	TOTAL INTEREST PAID OVER 30 YEARS
$136,000	8%	$998	$223,251
$150,000	7%	$998	$209,263
$166,000	6%	$995	$192,291

For the last twenty years, the mortgage interest rate averaged about 6.3 percent in both the United States and Canada.

As John and Elise McCaleb, first-time home buyers in Long Beach, California, point out: "You just have to jump in. There's no such thing as the right time or the right interest rate. If you try and wait until the market goes down, you'll get priced out." In the end, this last point is the most important: seldom, if ever, will a lower interest rate make up for a year's worth of lost equity buildup.

If you find yourself searching for your first home at a time of historically high interest rates, we want you to remember there will always be the opportunity to refinance when interest rates drop at some point in the future. For example, following the high mortgage interest rates in the 1980s (12 to 18 percent), there was massive mortgage refinancing when those rates dropped below 8 percent in the 1990s.

When applying for a mortgage, we want you to consider three factors that determine your interest rate. First, interest rates go through broad cycles tied to the federal government's fiscal policy. The second factor is your credit history, which most people won't be able to improve much in the short term. The third factor is the one over which you have the most control: the kind of mortgage you select.

The first factor, the interest rate, operates out of your control. It's just a condition of the current real estate market. You will simply look to find the best available mortgage interest rate. The second factor, your creditworthiness, is very important. Establishing and maintaining your credit rating is critical to your ability to qualify for the best interest rate. But some people, whose credit is still a work in progress, may still qualify for a loan, although it will probably have a higher-than-average interest rate. If you're in this predicament, you have two options: you can either accept the rate and work on improving your scores so you can refinance into a more favorable loan at some point in the future, or you can fix your credit before buying a home. Most lenders can put you in touch with a credit counselor who can help you improve your credit score in the most timely way.

If your credit score shows up low, it is highly recommended that you immediately check the report for mistakes. Errors are surprisingly common, and many can be cleaned up in a matter of months. If this is the case, you may want to straighten out your credit before looking seriously for a home. On pages 79–82 of this chapter, we'll take a look at some creative financing options that may be available to you if a low credit score has made conventional financing unattractive or unavailable.

The third factor that will impact your interest rate is whether you want a fixed-rate or adjustable-rate mortgage. For many years, nearly all mortgages were fixed rate, which meant the interest rate never changed over the life of the loan. A fixed-rate mortgage offers stability and the knowledge that your principal and interest payments won't change over time. This makes it a great choice when rates are at a low point because you can find a good rate, lock it in, and not worry about it going up. To give you a basis for comparison, consider that for the past twenty years mortgage rates in the United States and Canada have averaged roughly 7 percent (sources: Mortgage News Daily, 2010 and Canada Mortgage and Housing Corporation Data, 2010).

An adjustable-rate mortgage (commonly referred to as a variable-rate mortgage in Canada), or ARM, is a bit more complicated. The interest rates on ARMs are fixed for only a specified period, after which they rise and fall with changes in the market. For example, the rate on an ARM may be locked in for three years, after which it fluctuates every year thereafter. This kind of ARM is called a 3/1. In fact, there are almost as many varieties of ARM loans as there are apples at a supermarket. ARM loans can vary in how long their initial rate stays locked, how often they change, how much they change, and what rules they have.

The interest rates on adjustable-rate mortgages are tied to various financial indexes, such as the rate on U.S. Treasury Bills or six-month certificates of deposit (CDs). Similarly, in Canada the interest rates on variable-rate mortgages are based on the prime lending rate set by the Bank of Canada. Each ARM is based on one specific index onto which the lender adds a markup called a margin. For instance, if the rate on a six-month CD is 3 percent, and your ARM has a 2 percent margin on top of that index, your initial rate will be 5 percent. If at the end of your initial rate your base index has gone from 3 to 4 percent, your rate will move from 5 to 6 percent. Most ARMs offer some measure of protection through adjustment caps. If, for example, the CD rate jumped to 10 percent, your ARM would rocket up to 12 percent—unless you had an annual adjustment cap of, say, two points that kept your rate at only 7 percent. The same caps apply whether rates are rising or falling.

ARMs aren't for the risk averse. You would only want to secure an ARM loan for financing your home if you know the answers to these questions:

What is the teaser rate and how long will it last?
The teaser rate is typically a low promotional rate that usually lasts from six months to one year. Don't confuse this with the initial rate, which kicks in after the promotional rate expires. However, not all ARMs have teaser rates. (Teaser rates are not an issue on variable-rate mortgages in Canada.)

What is the initial rate and how long will it last?
This is your ARM's rate for the time it is fixed, which usually lasts somewhere between six months and seven years. Typically, the shorter the term, the lower the interest rate.

How often can the rate change?
After the initial period expires, the rate on your ARM will change at set intervals, usually every six months or one year in the United States. (Canadian rates can adjust on a monthly basis.) More frequent adjustments bring more risk, and usually a lower initial rate.

How much can it change with each adjustment?
Most ARM loans have a maximum number of percentage points they can move with each adjustment. This maximum is called a periodic cap.

In a worst-case scenario, how high could the rate go?

In the United States, ARM loans generally also have a lifetime cap, which is the highest the rate could ever go. (In Canada there is no lifetime cap, but the option to convert to a fixed-rate mortgage may be available at any time. Ask your mortgage specialist for details.)

Does it have a payment cap?

As the interest rate on your ARM rises, a payment cap limits the dollar amount you can pay each month. This sounds like a good thing, but it's not because it can lead to negative amortization, which occurs when any extra interest you can't pay is added to your principal debt, making it grow instead of shrink.

ARM loans should be approached with caution, especially if you think you'll live in your home a long time. Think of it this way: you're betting that rates will go down, or that you'll move or refinance before they move up significantly. As such, the ARM loans with the most tempting rates are those that adjust sooner and more frequently, and put you at the greatest risk. Regardless of your situation, if you're considering an ARM, we suggest you ask your lender to draw up a worst-case scenario so you know exactly how expensive your monthly payment could become and how quickly.

Now that we've brought the risks of an ARM to your attention, we should also point out that ARM loans can be useful. They make perfect sense when buyers have firm plans to move before the adjustments kick in. They can also be a good idea in a high interest-rate environment when the odds of rates dropping are in your favor. Our goal here is to provide you with the knowledge you need to make a well-informed mortgage decision with the help of your agent and lender.

Term

Another major factor, a mortgage loan's term, will determine how much interest you pay over the life of the loan and how quickly you build equity by paying down the loan. Most buyers in the United States still opt for a thirty-year mortgage. In Canada the majority of buyers favor a twenty-five-year amortization schedule with a variable-rate mortgage of five years. However, some see advantages to either shorter or longer terms. Shorter terms of either fifteen or twenty years are good for people who want to build equity quickly and who can afford a higher monthly payment. This dramatically reduces the amount of interest you pay over the life of the loan for two reasons. First, the interest is being charged over fifteen years rather than thirty. And second, fifteen-year loans usually offer a lower interest rate. The monthly payment on a fifteen-year loan will be higher than on a thirty-year loan, but not by as much as you might expect.

However, many buyers who like the idea of quickly building equity may still feel nervous about committing to the higher monthly payment of a shorter-term mortgage. We want you to know you can achieve similar results by taking out a thirty-year mortgage and paying a little extra toward the principal each month. Voluntary prepayment allows you to chip away at your principal faster and gives you more flexibility in case of a financial emergency by allowing you to elect not to pay the extra amount that month. If you choose this route, make sure that your loan does not come with prepayment penalties that would restrict you from doing this.

ADJUSTABLE-RATE MORTGAGE (ARM)

Imagine you're considering a 5/1, thirty-year ARM with a one-year teaser rate and a lifetime payment cap of 11 percent. After the teaser, the rate begins at an attractive 5 percent. Even with a two-point adjustment cap, however, a sudden rise in the index rate could more than double your rate—and your payment—in less than a decade.

RATE AND APPLICABLE YEARS	NO-CHANGE SCENARIO	WORST-CASE SCENARIO	WORST-CASE SCENARIO WITH TWO-POINT ADJUSTMENT CAP
Teaser Rate (Year 1)	$835 / month at 4%	$835 / month at 4%	$835 / month at 4%
Initial Rate (Years 2-5)	$939 / month at 5%	$939 / month at 5%	$939 / month at 5%
Adjustable Rate (Year 6)	$939 / month at 5%	$1,667 / month at 11%	$1,664 / month at 7%
Adjustable Rate (Year 7)	$939 / month at 5%	$1,667 / month at 11%	$1,408 / month at 9%
Adjustable Rate (Year 8)	$939 / month at 5%	$1,667 / month at 11%	$1,667 / month at 11%

An ARM may have a substantial impact on monthly payments: At 4 percent, a $175,000 mortgage = $835/month, while at 11 percent, a $175,000 mortgage = $1,667/month.

FIGURE 3.2

On the opposite end of the spectrum, in some markets lenders offer long-term loans such as a forty-year mortgage. Why? When you stretch the time over which you pay back your loan, each monthly payment will be lower. In most cases, this allows you to qualify for a higher-priced home. If you're considering a

DO THE MATH: FIND THE RIGHT MORTGAGE TERM

	15-YEAR	30-YEAR WITH ADDITIONAL $200 MONTHLY PRINCIPAL PREPAYMENT	30-YEAR	40-YEAR
Amount Borrowed	$175,000	$175,000	$175,000	$175,000
Interest Rate	7.5%	7.5%	7.5%	7.5%
Monthly Payment	$1,622	$1,424	$1,224	$1,151
Interest Paid Over Life of Loan	$117,009	$159,111	$265,505	$377,779
How It Stacks Up	A 15-year mortgage requires a higher monthly payment but dramatically reduces the amount you pay over the life of the loan. Plus, these mortgages usually come with a lower interest rate.	Voluntary prepayment on a 30-year mortgage essentially converts it to a 20-year while allowing you the flexibility to drop to the lower payment level if necessary.	The 30-year term is the most common in the industry. It offers reasonable monthly payments and a reasonable payoff time.	The 40-year mortgage allows you to stretch into a bigger house. Over time, however, the extra interest really adds up.

FIGURE 3.3

long-term mortgage loan, do the math to see how much that slightly lower monthly payment will cost you over the long haul. Frankly, while we typically don't recommend anything above thirty years for your first home-mortgage term, your individual needs may make this a perfectly acceptable option.

Understanding Your Monthly Payment

The bulk of your monthly payment will go toward paying off the principal and interest on your mortgage, which is amortized. Amortization is the process by which your lender calculates all the interest you will pay over the life of the loan, plus the amount you are borrowing, and divides that by the total number of payments you'll make (for example, a thirty-year loan is 360 monthly payments). Please note: even though every monthly principal and interest payment is exactly the same (based on the most popular thirty-year, fixed-rate loan), the proportion of principal and interest in each payment varies over time. In the beginning, the bulk of each payment will go toward interest; in later years, more of each payment will go toward paying off the principal (the amount you actually borrowed) thus accelerating your equity buildup.

On top of your principal and interest, each month you will probably pay a portion of your annual home owner's insurance premiums and property taxes, which most likely will change from year to year and thereby alter your monthly payment amount. For this reason, in the United States the monthly payment is often referred to as PITI (in Canada it could be referred to as PIT because insurance premiums are rarely included):

- Payments toward the **principal,** which reduces your loan amount
- **Interest,** which is paid to the lender for allowing you to borrow the money

- Property **taxes,** which are paid to local governments
- Home owner's **insurance,** which is paid to the company that is insuring your home against defined damages and liabilities

Understanding Amortization	
Principal loan amount:	$175,000
Interest rate:	6.5%
Interest accrued over 30 years:	$223,202
Total principal plus total interest:	$398,202
Divided by 360 monthly payments:	**$1,106**

Typically, buyers pay PITI (or PIT in Canada) to their lender in a single monthly payment. The insurance and tax portions of these funds are then held in escrow—a separate account—until the premiums or taxes are due. In other words, this escrow account works like withholding taxes from your paycheck. It allows you to save throughout the year so you'll be sure to have enough money to pay annual tax and insurance bills. It also assures the lender that these monies will be paid on time, that there will be no tax default, and that the lenders' investment (your home) will always be properly insured.

The Importance of Preapproval

Again, we recommend getting preapproved as soon as possible—definitely before you start looking at homes. It gives both you and the seller certainty that you can afford the property you want to buy, which can make all the difference in a multiple-offer situation. In surveys, many first-time buyers admit the most important thing they should have done was get preapproved sooner. Your real estate agent will ensure you don't put off this important step.

Loan officer Tommy Nelms of Austin, Texas, believes preapproval is even more critical due to occasional rapid shifts in the mortgage industry. To save time and energy, he suggests you speak with a loan officer before looking at homes. "It's imperative that buyers work with a lender so they know how much home they can afford before they get emotionally attached to one they can't," he says.

Get Preapproved—Not Just Prequalified

The terms are sometimes used interchangeably, but prequalification and preapproval are NOT the same.

Prequalification is the process by which a loan officer estimates the amount you can borrow based on information you provide about your income, assets, and debts. There is no formal application or verification of that information, so it is only a rough estimate.

Preapproval, on the other hand, involves a formal application that goes through underwriting for independent verification of the information you provide. It is the same loan approval process that all buyers must go through, except that preapproval gets it out of the way before you find the house you want to buy. Upon preapproval, you will receive a formal commitment from the lender stating how much you can borrow and at what rate.

DECIDE AMONG YOUR MORTGAGE OPTIONS

A down payment, an interest rate, and the time over which you pay back your loan—that's the basic recipe for a mortgage loan. Even though all mortgages have the same ingredients, you can combine them in a myriad of ways to fit your financial needs. We hope you remember that the kind of mortgage you choose will shape how much you pay up front, how much you pay each month, and how much interest you pay over the life of the loan. You decide which of these factors is most important to you:

I want a low monthly payment

There are two fundamental ways to achieve a low monthly payment: you buy less home or put more down up front. Most people choose the latter. A larger down payment will reduce your total loan amount and may secure a better interest rate. Depending on where interest rates are, your long-term plans, and how you feel about risk, you might also consider an adjustable-rate mortgage or one with a longer term.

I want to put as little down as possible

If you have only a little cash to spend, see if a piggyback (or second mortgage) loan is available, such as an 80-10-10 or 80-15-5. Remember, however, a lower down payment will come with a higher interest rate, a higher monthly payment, and more interest over the life of the loan.

I want to build up equity quickly

Consider a loan amortized over fifteen or twenty years, or take out a thirty-year mortgage and make voluntary prepayments. These are also good choices if you value paying less interest over the life of the loan and building up the equity you have in the home. This can positively impact your financial net worth and your creditworthiness.

I want to minimize risk

A thirty-year fixed-rate loan with a 20 percent down payment is probably your safest option in the United States. You move in with equity already in the property, and your interest rate is locked in for the life of the loan, no matter how high interest rates may climb after you move in. (If you live in Canada, we advise you to discuss your loan options with your mortgage specialist to minimize risk.)

Remember, as a first-time home buyer, we urge you to consider all your options carefully, including government-sponsored first-time buyer programs. We think you'll enjoy the benefits these programs offer and thank yourself for years to come.

CREATIVE FINANCING

The evolving consumer lending landscape at times makes conventional financing somewhat more difficult, expensive, or perhaps altogether unavailable. So, as an option, we'd like to introduce a set of time-tested financing strategies that may be available to you regardless of unfavorable economic circumstances, whether general or personal.

Creative financing incorporates a set of strategies that can help you buy a property with less of your own money used as a down payment and may even lower your monthly payment. A common creative financing scenario involves a seller with a specific situation that may work to your advantage such as a high equity position in the seller's home and a need to sell. The situation presents a unique opportunity in which you and your real estate agent construct a creative transaction that meets the seller's goals and still works for you.

The following four examples represent common ways to execute creative financing. First, a seller may offer owner financing. In this case, the seller actually holds the mortgage for you while you make payments. A second situation involves your assumption of the seller's mortgage. In this scenario, the seller's mortgage lender allows you, the buyer, to take responsibility for the seller's mortgage. A third situation is called a wrap finance, where the owner offers you a new loan while keeping and paying down the original loan (the new loan "wraps" the seller's original loan). The fourth concept is a lease option in which you lease the property from the seller until you have the equity or cash to buy it. If you're challenged to find financing through conventional means, you might consider ways you can employ creative financing to help you achieve your home purchase.

While owner financing is widely available, please note that not all mortgages are assumable and many mortgages have a "due on sale" clause that will involve the lender's notification and approval for one to be assumed or wrapped. Be aware that some areas don't permit lease options or their variations: deed-for-contract and lease purchase. We recommend you ask your agent to connect you with a reputable real estate attorney if you choose one of those creative-financing options.

Figure 3.4 shows how the numbers might work in a scenario where you attempt to take ownership of a $100,000 property through creative financing. You'll note that conventional financing (column 1) is included as a point of reference.

BASIC CREATIVE FINANCING FOR PROPERTY ACQUISITIONS

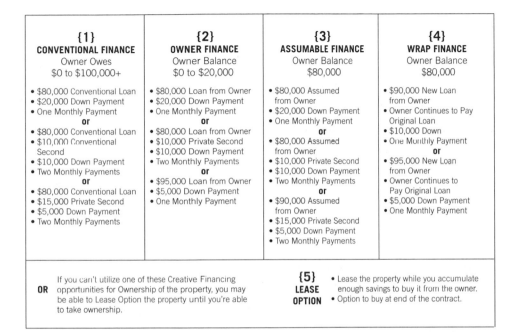

{1} **CONVENTIONAL FINANCE** Owner Owes $0 to $100,000+	{2} **OWNER FINANCE** Owner Balance $0 to $20,000	{3} **ASSUMABLE FINANCE** Owner Balance $80,000	{4} **WRAP FINANCE** Owner Balance $80,000
• $80,000 Conventional Loan • $20,000 Down Payment • One Monthly Payment **or** • $80,000 Conventional Loan • $10,000 Conventional Second • $10,000 Down Payment • Two Monthly Payments **or** • $80,000 Conventional Loan • $15,000 Private Second • $5,000 Down Payment • Two Monthly Payments	• $80,000 Loan from Owner • $20,000 Down Payment • One Monthly Payment **or** • $80,000 Loan from Owner • $10,000 Private Second • $10,000 Down Payment • Two Monthly Payments **or** • $95,000 Loan from Owner • $5,000 Down Payment • One Monthly Payment	• $80,000 Assumed from Owner • $20,000 Down Payment • One Monthly Payment **or** • $80,000 Assumed from Owner • $10,000 Private Second • $10,000 Down Payment • Two Monthly Payments **or** • $90,000 Assumed from Owner • $15,000 Private Second • $5,000 Down Payment • Two Monthly Payments	• $90,000 New Loan from Owner • Owner Continues to Pay Original Loan • $10,000 Down • One Monthly Payment **or** • $95,000 New Loan from Owner • Owner Continues to Pay Original Loan • $5,000 Down Payment • One Monthly Payment

OR If you can't utilize one of these Creative Financing opportunities for Ownership of the property, you may be able to Lease Option the property until you're able to take ownership.	{5} **LEASE OPTION** • Lease the property while you accumulate enough savings to buy it from the owner. • Option to buy at end of the contract.

FIGURE 3.4

In all four of the ownership scenarios (columns 1-4), it is important you understand that a private second loan can also come from the seller. Just know that secondary liens in general carry less favorable terms for the buyer—it's about collateral. First liens are generally secured against the property and first in line if the deal goes sour and the property must be liquidated to pay back the loan. Secondary lenders account for this in the terms they offer. The main thing to recognize is the many financing options you have when buying a home. Sometimes you just need to look in less obvious places to find them.

Canadian agent Sylvie Begin of Ottawa, Ontario, did just that. Her clients were second- and third-year medical students who had rented a place for several years, one they absolutely loved. "At the time, they earned a modest student salary and really couldn't qualify for a conventional mortgage," Sylvie recalls. "They were about to start their medical careers and knew they'd be making much more money in a few years, so future income really wasn't a concern."

Sylvie's clients wanted to stop wasting money on rent, so creative financing made perfect sense. And the seller, who was the clients' landlord at the time, was happy to work with them. After agreeing on a price with the seller, Sylvie negotiated a lease option purchase in which her clients would pay a few hundred dollars extra each month in addition to rent. The seller/landlord held the extra money, and it accumulated as an eventual down payment. Sylvie adds, "The key for my clients was to agree on a price with the seller, especially in a scenario where the real estate market might be flat or depreciating in a year or two."

Both parties agreed on the amount of a nonrefundable deposit check, which guaranteed the buyers an option—an exclusive right to purchase the property at the agreed-upon price in a predetermined time period. The parties also agreed on the option expiration date. Every piece was negotiated, including the portion of the rent that went toward the down payment.

YOUR LENDER DECIDES WHAT YOU CAN BORROW
BUT YOU DECIDE WHAT YOU CAN AFFORD

Olivia and Alex each earn $4,000 a month. Tradition-ally, their maximum housing payments would be 28 percent of their incomes, or $1,120.

However, their financial profiles are really very different, leading them to very different decisions about how much they can afford.

Olivia has $15,000 in student loans, just bought a new car, and has several credit cards with balances.

Car payment	$350
Student loans	$150
Credit card minimum	+ $150
Monthly nonhousing debt	$650
Maximum total debt payment (36 percent of $4,000)	$1,440
	− $650
Safe housing payment	$790

Alex's student loans are paid off, he has little credit card debt, and his car is an economy model.

Car payment	$200
Credit card minimum	+ $50
Monthly nonhousing debt	$250
Maximum total debt payment (36 percent of $4,000)	$1,440
	− $250
Safe housing payment	$1,190

FIGURE 3.5

They closed about eighteen months later and the home was theirs. "It was a win-win deal for both my clients and the seller," Sylvie notes. "All elements were agreed upon in advance, and the tenants, my clients, always had the ability to opt out at any time by giving up a nonrefundable deposit and any extra payments made toward the property."

THE SUITCASE PRINCIPLE

Imagine you're packing to go on vacation. You get out your suitcase and start filling it with T-shirts and shorts, your toothbrush and swimsuit, and a nice outfit in case you go out for a formal dinner. You pack everything you know you'll need to make your vacation as fun as possible. However, you probably won't pack the suitcase so tight you have to sit on it to get it closed. You know that once you get to Boise or Bali, you'll probably find something you want to bring home. So, you leave room for the unknown.

The suitcase principle applies just as well to mortgages. When you get your preapproval letter, make sure the monthly payment is an amount you feel comfortable paying each month. Lenders are careful, but they make qualification decisions based on averages and formulas. They won't understand the nuances of your lifestyle and spending patterns quite as well as you do. So, leave a little room in your suitcase for the unexpected—for all the new opportunities your home will give you to spend money, from furnishing the guest bedroom to landscaping the lawn. "You don't want to be so strapped that you can't go out and buy a flat of flowers," says Mary Anne Collins, an agent in California. "You want to be able to afford the things that make a house a home. If you max out what a loan originator says you can afford, you might not be able to do that."

As a general rule, we recommend spending no more than a third of your gross monthly income on your first home payment. Historically, banks used a ratio called 28/36 to decide how much buyers could borrow. An approved housing payment couldn't be more than 28 percent of the buyer's gross monthly income, and his or her total debt load, including car payments, student loans, and credit card payments, couldn't be more than 36 percent. (In Canada lenders apply similar formulas to determine how much a buyer can afford. The Gross Debt Service ratio, or GDS, is not to exceed 32 percent of the buyer's gross monthly income, and the Total Debt Service ratio, or TDS, is not to exceed 43 percent of the buyer's total debt load.) As home prices have risen, some lenders have responded by stretching these ratios to as high as 50 percent. No matter how expensive your market, though, we urge you to think carefully before stretching your personal budget quite so much.

Deciding how much you can afford should involve some attention to how your financial profile will change in the coming years. If you expect to incur a bunch of new costs—for example, if you plan to start a family—it might be smart to scale back. On the other hand, if you're about to get a big promotion, make your final car payment, or send a child from private day care into public kindergarten, you may be able to afford a little more. In the long run, your own peace of mind and financial security will matter most.

Finding the right mortgage takes a little work, but you'll find that the effort is well worth it. Chosen wisely, your home mortgage can be one of your best financial assets. It's what enables you to fulfill the dream of home ownership. It helps ensure your financial security through building equity and net worth. As your equity grows, it will be a valuable source of creditworthiness and financial stability.

Notes to Take Home

- Follow these six steps to financing your home:
  1. Choose a loan officer.
  2. Make a loan application and get preapproved.
  3. Determine what you want to pay and select a loan option.
  4. Submit to the lender an accepted purchase offer contract.
  5. Get an appraisal and title commitment.
  6. Obtain funding at closing.

- You don't need to save up a lot of money for the down payment. A conventional mortgage can require as little as a 5 percent down payment. Some programs may require less.

- Having the right loan officer (or mortgage specialist) working for you assures that all the details will be handled in an accurate and timely manner and that you will receive sound financial advice.

- Remember, lenders determine what you can borrow, but only you can decide what you can afford.

- Understanding the three basic parts of a mortgage loan—down payment, interest rate, and terms—will help you choose the best one for you.

- Visit YourFirstHomeBook.com for worksheets and other resources.

MARY'S FIRST HOME

   The first fourteen years of my life seemed idyllic. My family lived in a wonderful home in Greeley, Colorado. I was the middle child of five. Then one day our lives changed dramatically. My father was injured in a major automobile accident and unable to work, and we had to sell our home and move into a rental. It was a sad day when we packed up and left the home we loved.

Having been through such an ordeal, you can imagine how my father felt when, at the age of twenty-nine, I purchased a home for the enormous sum of $52,000—a lot of money back in 1975. Still somewhat distressed, he told me I was making the biggest mistake of my life.

At the time my husband and I lived in an apartment two blocks from a California beach after spending a year traveling around the country in a motor home. My son was one year old, and I was pregnant with my daughter. I was determined that my kids would have a home with a yard where they could play barefoot in the grass. We found exactly what we had in mind: a two-story home close to the beach with a park and elementary school nearby. It had a huge backyard just as I had imagined.

We had no savings, but we purchased the home using my husband's Veteran Administration benefits. We still had to sell one of our cars to make the down payment. I didn't care because having that home far outweighed any inconvenience. I had a bike outfitted so I could carry both my babies to the grocery store and travel around the neighborhood.

I was so thrilled to move into our first home that even as pregnant as I was, I went to work knocking out the wall between the dining room and living room, redoing the fireplace, wallpapering the bedrooms, painting the upstairs, and landscaping. My daughter came two weeks later. I loved bringing her home from the hospital to the room I had decorated for her.

Even today, that first home means more to me than anything I've purchased since. It was our children's first home, where we put down roots for the first time and really felt secure. My husband built a gazebo in the backyard and I made even more improvements, putting up shutters and planting two magnolia trees in the front lawn.

I remember one of the real estate agents we interviewed when we began our search told me that the mature thing would be to go home and save some money, and then we'd talk. Thank goodness we didn't listen. We sold that California house for $76,000 a year after we bought it and used the profit to finance our dream: a home on a Colorado mountaintop.

I think having a home means more to me and my siblings because we know what it feels like to lose a home we loved. Today, every one of us owns a beautiful home. And although it took awhile, my parents were finally able to buy another home, which they eventually owned free and clear.

Mary Tennant is a board member of Keller Williams Realty, Inc.

CHAPTER 4:
FIND YOUR HOME

· · · · ·

When Cheri Corrado was looking for her first home, she thought she knew exactly what she wanted. She was a real estate agent, after all, and knew her Washington, DC, market inside out. She also "knew" she wanted a detached single-family home, not one of the townhomes common in her area. She searched for weeks, fruitlessly, before a chance conversation with another agent at her office changed everything.

"I was just telling her about the trouble I was having," says Cheri, "and she asked, 'Well, why do you want a single-family house?'"

Cheri thought about it and was stunned to realize that she didn't want a single-family home. She didn't particularly like yard work and didn't have time for it anyway. What she wanted, she discovered, was as much square footage as possible. She had assumed that detached single-family homes would get her the most space.

Once I realized that what I most wanted about a home was size, I could stop looking for a detached home and start looking for size," she says. She soon found a townhome she absolutely loved. "That's why you need to get down to why you want what you want because there may be another way of getting it."

You may think that shopping for homes starts with jumping in the car and driving all over town. And it's true that hopping in the car to go look is probably the most exciting part of the home-buying process. All those properties! All those neighborhoods! All those choices! However, driving around is fun for only so long—if weeks go by without finding what you're looking for, the fun can fade pretty fast. That's why we say that looking for homes begins with carefully assessing your values, wants, and needs, both for the short and long terms. "I encourage my first-time buyers to dream a little bit. I ask them to step into an imaginative space, to think about what they really want and need, and to consider what will make them happy as first-time buyers. This is about their dreams," says Canadian agent Rick Brash.

Abraham Lincoln once said that if he had eight hours in which to cut down a tree, he would spend six sharpening his axe. In the home-buying process, consultation with your agent is your way to sharpen the axe. You may think you already have a pretty good idea of what your first home might look like, and you're probably right. However, you want to be sure you haven't missed something. Remember, as Cheri Corrado learned, you can't be absolutely sure what you really need until you take the time to get down to the "why."

GOING FROM "WHAT" TO "WHY"

When we say you need to get down to the "why," that's another way of saying you need to figure out what you value most and how your first home can embody those values. In a way, it's a little like sending your expectations to boot camp: you want to tear them down so you can put them back together in a new way. During your consultation, we challenge you to set aside any preconceptions you may have about what you want and the homes that are available. Then, beginning with a clean slate, you should assemble a list of search criteria that reflects what you truly need and every reasonable alternative for fulfilling those needs.

First, let's clear up a definition. By "values," we mean those broad, overarching considerations that are the bedrock of your personal desires—privacy, safety, good schools, time outdoors, entertaining at home, and enough space. Your values shape your specific needs—a large yard, room to entertain, or short commute. Most specific of all will be your "wants." They will be the particular ways you'd like to meet your needs. For example, you may have a specific neighborhood in mind to fulfill your need for a short commute. Or, your wants may be things you just plain like, such as granite countertops or a fence for privacy.

Now, we would like you to take out a piece of paper and write down everything you want in a home. Everything you can think of: size, neighborhood, architectural style, amenities, everything. Once you have the list of "whats," you can start getting down to the "whys."

Here's how this process might work. Let's say that right at the top of your list is your desire to live in the Southwest Woods neighborhood. Nowhere else will do. Unfortunately, Southwest Woods is so very expensive that the only thing you could afford to buy there would be a home barely big enough for you and your cat Stanley, let alone your spouse and future kids. As you sit at your kitchen table between your spouse and agent, with Stanley purring on your lap, your agent asks why you want to live in that particular neighborhood. "I just really like Southwest Woods," you say. "It's where I've always dreamed of living."

DETERMINING YOUR NEEDS: FINDING A WIN-WIN SOLUTION

QUESTION: DO I NEED A FENCE?

Darren wants a home with a fence. Anna, his colleague, also wants a home with a fence. But they have different reasons.

CONSULTATION

Darren has two big dogs he wants to keep outside. Anna wants privacy.

WIN-WIN SOLUTION

Darren's home will fulfill this need if it has:
- a fence, OR
- a seller willing to pay for a fence, OR
- a final sales price that leaves money to pay for a fence on his own.

Anna's home will fulfill this need if it has:
- a fence, OR
- a fence allowance, OR
- many trees, OR
- a location on a hill or on a very large lot.

"What is it about Southwest Woods that you like?" your agent asks. "Is it close to your work? Does it have special amenities?"

"None of that," you say. "It's actually a little inconvenient. I just love all the trees and historic houses. It's the kind of neighborhood I've always liked."

In this case, the "what" of Southwest Woods leads to the "why": you like older, wooded neighborhoods. Once you realize that, your agent can suggest alternative ways to meet that need. Perhaps your agent could introduce you to Northeast Knoll, where the homes aren't quite as big, but where the streets are quiet, the lawns are shady, and the whole place feels a lot like a scaled-down Southwest Woods.

As you explore your needs, be sure to separate them into immediate, short-term needs and anticipated future needs, such as room to start a family or a new home business. In North America, people tend to move every six or seven years.

So, it's very likely that some of your long-term wants can move off your list in the short term.

Here's how that might work: let's back up for a second and imagine that you have a different reason for wanting Southwest Woods. "It's the neighborhood with the very best schools in the entire state," you tell your agent.

"How old are your children?" your agent asks. You say you don't have any yet. You say you're waiting for now. In this case, you actually couldn't care less about tall trees and old homes. What you are really valuing is education, and you see a Southwest Woods address as a way to achieve that.

But notice that you don't need great schools today. At the least, it'll be five years before you have a child in school. In a situation like this, you might consider whether this is the home you expect to live in when that want turns into a need. If it is, then Southwest Woods clearly may be your best option for right now. If not, maybe you should put your more immediate needs at the top of the list.

In short, we think your consultation session starts with your values. From there, you can explore your wants and needs. Once you understand that, you're ready to go back to the "what": your final list of criteria.

GOING FROM "WHY" BACK TO "WHAT"

This is the point at which many home-buying books would offer an exhaustive list of possible features and characteristics to consider when shopping for a home. We're not going to do that. We believe it will be best for you to focus on the options within your own local market, rather than trying to make sense of hard-and-fast rules that are supposed to apply everywhere. They never do. Instead, we offer questions that help you evaluate and prioritize the things you want and need from your first home. Remember our goal: to help you define the criteria that will find you a home that meets all your needs and as many of your wants as possible.

What do I want my home to be close to? What do I want my neighborhood to be like?

There are two ways to think about location: proximity and character. Proximity means the spots on the map that are geographically desirable to you: they're close to your job, your friends and family, and city amenities, among other things. However, the question of location also encompasses character: the kind of homes, streets, and parks that a given area has to offer. For example, you may want a downtown condo because you like the bustle of urban life, not because the area is close to anything in particular. Someone else may want an older home and be willing to look in any part of town as long as it's historic.

So, when you discuss location with your agent, we advise you to separate proximity from character so you can better prioritize your needs. Some people may be willing to drive farther to work so they can live in that historic neighborhood on the hill. Others want the fastest commute possible so they can get home to their families.

Canadian agent Zan Molko of Toronto, Ontario, explores the geographic needs of his buyers in literal terms. "I sit down with my clients and we look at a large map of the city. I ask them to balance location with affordability." As they talk, Zan learns about his clients' specific needs and wants, while his clients learn more about the realities of the market. Armed with a clearer perspective, his clients can undertake a more targeted home search and make a more informed buying decision.

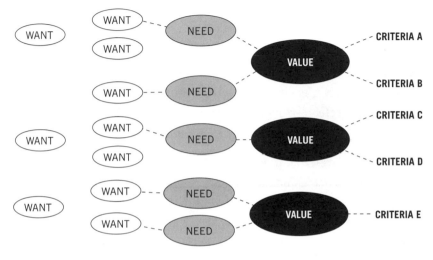

FIGURE 4.1

How much space do I need? What do I need that space for?

It's not enough to say that you want a four-bedroom home. A 1,200-square-foot four-bedroom ranch built in 1950 will offer far less space than a more contemporary four-bedroom home that could easily have double the square footage. A smaller home may be a fine starter home for a family with a baby on the way that needs only a nursery and perhaps a toddler's bedroom before moving up to another, bigger property. However, it would be a poor choice if you're planning to stay there so long that your growing family will start bouncing off the walls.

While many people judge space by the number of bedrooms, it's important to think carefully about what you want the space for. Maybe you like to entertain, and a wide-open floor plan is more important than extra bedrooms. Or, maybe you want room for a home office—and a converted basement or garage could do the trick as well as an extra bedroom. So, the question of size encompasses both how much and what kind of space you need.

What is most important: location or size?

The nicer the neighborhood, the more expensive the homes. Everyone knows that. Most first-time buyers usually have to settle for a trade-off between size and location. Some people may prefer a smaller home in a nicer area, while others would rather have more square footage, even if the neighborhood's not quite as upscale.

Would I be interested in a fixer-upper?

One possible way to get as much space as you want in the neighborhood you love is by taking on a fixer-upper. Transforming a run-down property from eyesore to eye-opener can be financially and personally rewarding. However, before you add "poor condition" to your list of criteria, we want you to make sure you know what you're getting into. First, recognize that a fixer-upper isn't necessarily a deal if you end up putting more money into the repairs than you saved on the purchase price. Buying a property in poor condition may be a longer, more complicated process as you call in specialists for estimates on what it will cost to update that 1970s kitchen, fix the foundation, or put in new floors. If you don't have the time, patience, or talent for this project, you may not be happy taking on the home-improvement challenge.

How important is appreciation?

Another way to get as much as possible in the neighborhood you really want is through strategic equity buildup. That is, rather than buying in the neighborhood you love today, it might be smart to buy a fast-appreciating starter home and use your equity to make the leap a few years down the road. In the Seattle, Washington, area, for example, the most affordable homes are on the far-flung edges of town. Agent Roy Van Winkle often suggests that even people who hate long commutes consider the value of outlying properties, many of which are appreciating faster than urban homes. "You can put up with the commute for a couple of years, and then use your equity to buy a place in Seattle," he often tells them. So, a few years of living somewhere less-than-perfect can often be a great way to end up where you really want to be.

How important is neighborhood stability?

Neighborhoods change over time. New developments, roads, or revitalization programs can affect traffic patterns, commute times, and your home's resale value. If you're buying a starter home, you might not have to worry much about what the neighborhood will look like in ten or fifteen years. However, if you're planning on staying put, your home search criteria should include some attention to development patterns that will help your neighborhood hold or increase in value.

Would I be interested in a condo?

Around 90 percent of all homes sold are what agents call a "detached, single-family residence." In plain English, that's what most people call "a house." But a house isn't the only choice available, and many buyers find that condos (or their related ilk, such as townhomes) fit perfectly into their lifestyles or finances.

Many people think of condos as downtown high-rises. However, the term "condominium" doesn't refer to a particular kind of construction. Instead, the term refers to a form of shared ownership. When you buy a condo, you're buying your own space within a building. And when we say "space," we mean space: condo owners usually do not actually own the walls, floor, or ceiling—they own the space inside. Maintenance costs are shared, and maintenance headaches are handled by a board of directors elected by the condo members. (Condo ownership specifications and maintenance regulations vary from area to area, so consult your agent for more information.)

Condos are great for people who don't want the hassles of home maintenance. Some people dislike yard work or simply like the idea of belonging to a community. Many condos also have amenities like swimming pools and playgrounds that many single-family homes lack. And even though on average, condos may cost slightly more per square foot than detached single-family homes, in many cities condos are among the most affordable properties on the market.

Condos aren't for everyone. For one thing, they have rules, usually called CC&Rs (for covenants, codes, and restrictions). CC&Rs vary from community to community: they may govern pets, how many vehicles you can have, what you can store on your patio, or how much noise you can make. So, before you commit to a condo, make sure you can live with the rules. Also make sure you understand the fees, which cover the maintenance, the general property insurance, and upkeep of things such as the plumbing or the roof. Remember the flip side of not having to deal with maintenance? You have very little control—if the rest of the members decide to let the property slide into disrepair, there's not much you can do but try to sell before it's too late. And it would be the same situation if they agree to levy an assessment to all owners to cover a major requisition or improvement project.

Would I be interested in new home construction?
For some buyers, nothing but brand-new will do. However, new home construction comes with some special concerns. On one hand, new homes have the latest features and floor plans, so you don't have to worry about old appliances or outdated bathrooms. They're often the best way to maximize square footage. Frequently, you get to customize your home's décor, and new

subdivisions often have amenities like swimming pools, parks, running trails, and security gates, which older neighborhoods may lack.

On the other hand, like condos, about 80 percent of new developments in the United States require buyers to join and pay fees toward a home owner's association. That means living by the CC&Rs. Many people appreciate these rules because they protect property values by keeping the neighborhood tidy and pleasant. However, some home owners find them nit-picky and annoying—disputes over community rules have even led to lawsuits over residents' rights to fly a flag, put in a doghouse, or display political signs, to name just a few examples.

If a brand-new home is a top priority, that will shape your search for a location. We want to point out that the newest homes are almost always on the outskirts of town, which may be convenient if you work in a suburban office park but may be excruciating if your job is downtown. Also, it has implications if you plan to move. Like condos that lose their luster when a newer building goes in next door, it can sometimes be hard to sell a gently used home when buyers have the alternative of a new one in the next subdivision down the road.

What features do I need? What amenities do I want?

Your lifestyle determines the kind of features you really need your home to have. If you have four kids, you need a lot of bedrooms; if you have four Alaskan Malamutes, you need a big yard. You might need a living area big enough for a grand piano, wide doorways to accommodate a wheelchair, enough bathrooms for litter boxes for all the cats, and a big garage for the car collection. For some buyers, spiritual concerns also come into play. "When I work with buyers from some cultures, many want homes that face a certain way, or whose address adds up to a certain number," says agent Elaine Sans Souci.

ANALYZE WHAT YOU WANT AND WHAT YOU NEED IN A HOME'S FEATURES AND AMENITIES

Features

- Age: Do you prefer historic properties, or newer ones?
- Style: Do you have a special preference for ranches, bungalows, or another style of construction?
- Bedrooms: How many?
- Bathrooms: How many? Are they updated?
- Living and Dining Areas: A traditional, formal layout, or a more open, contemporary plan?
- Stories: How many?
- Square feet: How much space?
- Ceilings: How high?
- Kitchen: How big? Recently updated? Open to the other living areas?
- Storage: Big closets, a shed, an extra-large garage?
- Parking: A garage or carport? Room for how many cars?
- Extras: Attic or basement?

Amenities

- Office
- Play/exercise room
- Security system
- Sprinkler
- Workshop/studio
- In-law suite
- Fireplace
- Pool
- Hot tub
- Sidewalk
- Wooded lot
- Patio, deck, or porch
- Laundry room

Homes come with a dizzying variety of features and amenities—that's what makes searching for the right one so much fun! Your dream home may have high ceilings or wood floors, luxurious carpets or big windows, a pool or a fireplace, vintage or flashy countertops. But, as you're envisioning all the wonderful things you want your home to have, we want you to be very careful to separate those that you truly need—like those four bedrooms—from those you could do without. Most homes simply won't have it all. For example, if your list of wants includes a home that is both a historic property and has a wide-open layout with plenty of storage, you may be in trouble. In many areas, older homes were built for older lifestyles, which usually meant smaller closets and bathrooms, and usually a more formal layout with distinct living, dining, and kitchen areas. So, you'll have to decide what you value most—the age or the contemporary layout.

What does your home need now, and what does it need the potential for?

There are some things you can't change about a property, such as its age or location, and some that are expensive to change, such as its size or layout. Still, there is much about a home that is fluid. As you're deciding which of your wants are true needs, remember Wini and Stanley in Levittown: part of the joy of owning your own home is being able to keep making it better and better. Some of your needs, then, will be things the home doesn't have to have today—but has to have the potential for. Maybe you don't need a home with lush landscaping, for example, but you do need a yard with good light and room to put in a garden. Maybe you don't need a big, screened-in porch right now, but you do need a layout and lot that would work with the porch or deck you someday hope to add. So, we encourage you to make a special list of needs for "potential" — potential for the pool, the renovated gourmet kitchen, the master bedroom suite, or whatever else your long-term plans entail.

Of all your wants and needs, which are the most important?

As you can clearly see, you'll need to prioritize. Your needs come first, of course, but then you should sort through your wants and decide which are the most important. We suggest you don't take anything off the list—your agent should know to keep an eye out for those granite countertops or built-in bookshelves that make you swoon. But your focus should be on the "must-haves," with the "want-to-haves" or the "nice-to-haves" coming later.

Kailey Humphries and her husband were aspiring first-time home buyers in Calgary, Alberta, with a unique need for space. Working with their agent, Debbie Komitsch, they had been looking for a few months. They knew they wanted a townhome-style property. And while they were willing to compromise on certain aspects of their first

Your Home Wants and Needs Criteria

- Location
- Size
- Condition
- Appreciation
- Neighborhood

- Freestanding or condo/townhome, resale or new construction
- Features and amenities
- Potential for expansion or improvement

home, they really needed all the free storage space they could find.

"My husband and I are members of the Canadian National Bobsled Team, so we have a lot of equipment and we needed space for it. We knew a garage or a basement was a necessity," Kailey recalls. After their need for storage space, location was their next priority. Since their training facility and work location are in the same area, they didn't want a long commute to either site.

"We were not too picky on the overall size of the place, but we ideally wanted two bedrooms, two bathrooms, and a garage for storage close to where we trained and worked." Debbie found them the perfect solution—a 1,200-square-foot home with two bedrooms, two and a half bathrooms, and a single car garage. "And within ten minutes of where we train and work!" says Kailey.

YOU KNOW WHAT YOU WANT AND NEED . . . NOW WHAT?

As you can see, there are many factors to consider when setting your criteria. But even after you've figured out what you want to spend, what you're looking for, and where you're willing to compromise, there's one more thing you want to know: What happens next? What will be the process for your home search and for making an offer?

So, before you leave this initial consultation, ask your agent for the next steps to finding a home that fits your criteria and timetable as soon as possible. That means asking:

What kind of home to search for?

Ask your agent to reiterate what you're looking for so you can clarify any points of confusion.

How you'll be notified of new properties?

You may get a daily e-mail, or you may get a phone call a few times a week. Find out how and when you can expect to be informed.

What are the rules of your local real estate market?

You need to be prepared for the offer process before you find a home you love. This is particularly important if you're in a hot market where you may need to act quickly.

SIZING UP HOMES

Searching for homes is a little like dating: you have a pretty good idea what will make a good match, but you never know exactly when the sparks will fly. You might spend a few weeks combing the market, or you might fall in love your first trip out. No matter how long it takes or how many stops on your journey, getting the right home under contract is essentially a three-step process:

1. Check out homes that match your criteria.

2. Write and negotiate an offer on the right home.

3. Inspect the property before finalizing the deal.

At the end, you can take the optional fourth step of breathing a big sigh of relief because once you and the seller have agreed on a final contract, you're in the home stretch.

It's the big day: your first trip to see homes. You meet with your agent, Cindy, to review the list of homes she picked out of the MLS (Multiple Listing Service) based on your personal criteria, and then you head to the first property. Cindy opens the door, and you both step inside. What happens next is a team effort.

What You See

You've just arrived at 123 Mockingbird Lane. From the MLS printout, you know it's got three bedrooms and two baths, just like you wanted. From the sidewalk, it looks fantastic. As you step into the living room, you're immediately wowed by the fireplace and its classy stone hearth. You mentally arrange your furniture and decide your couch would fit perfectly against the side wall. As you move to the kitchen, you note that it's open and spacious, but you also wonder if there's enough counter space for the high-intensity cooking you love. Walking through the bedrooms, you think they seem a little small, but that master bedroom has a great

WHAT YOU SEE . . . AND WHAT YOUR AGENT KNOWS

YOUR JOB is to see how the home stacks up to your wants and needs.

Questions YOU answer:

1. Does it have the right space and layout for my lifestyle?
2. Does it offer value to me?
3. Is the location convenient to my job and my kids' schools?
4. Does it have features and amenities I like?

YOUR AGENT'S JOB is to know how the home stacks up to its competition.

Questions YOUR AGENT answers:

1. Does its size and layout compare well to others around it?
2. Does it offer value in relation to other homes around it?
3. Will the location hold its value?
4. Does it show signs of major maintenance or structural concerns?

walk-in closet and a nice view of the yard. As you head back downstairs, you think you might really like it—but it's your first home to visit so you're not quite sure.

What Your Agent Knows

Your agent follows you inside. Having previewed the home before showing it to you, Cindy knows the fireplace is beautiful but also knows that most of the homes in the subdivision have them. When she worked her way through the house, she looked for telltale signs of disrepair. Cindy hadn't seen any stains on the ceiling, so she's thinking there hasn't been any major leaks. However, she had seen some slight cracks around some of the windows, and one of the doors had stuck. This told her the foundation could become a problem down the road. She knows the yard is bigger than most of the ones nearby and has especially elaborate landscaping.

Comparing Notes

Above all, your property should be right for you, however offbeat and funky your tastes may be. Remember, though, that someday you will have to sell this home to someone else, and in the meantime you'll have to deal with maintenance. If your agent strongly cautions you against a particular home, we urge you to pay attention. If you had decided that Mockingbird Lane was the right home for you, for example, Cindy would have cautioned you that foundation problems could crop up at some point and encouraged an inspection before you made an offer. Even if you don't mind a sticking door or two, the next buyer might. "I want to be excited with you, but I'm also looking at our relationship," says Austin, Texas, agent David Raesz. "In five or seven years when you're ready to sell, I don't want you saying I got you into something I can't get you out of."

Refine As You Go

Every property teaches you something. As your search progresses and your knowledge grows, tap into these new insights to continually refine your criteria. Imagine, for example, that you decided to look for homes in the Mockingbird Lane area because of its convenient location, even though the homes are a little smaller and older than you'd like. Then, after looking at a dozen homes in the area, you realize they all share the same flaw—they're all just a little too small. Maybe it's time for you to reshuffle your priorities and consider a longer commute in order to buy a bigger, newer home. These kinds of refinements are perfectly normal. In fact, they enhance your search as you share them with your agent and use them to better focus on the right property for you.

There are also some helpful things you can do while you evaluate homes during your search. After a day or two of looking at several properties, it can become hard to remember which homes were more appealing and why. In fact, after viewing numerous homes in a few hours, they can become one big blur.

To help you remember each home distinctly, take along a notepad and write down the address of each property you visit before you get out of the car. While you tour the home, take short notes about the things you like and don't like and note a distinguishing feature (for example, a purple birdhouse or a stained-glass window) that will jog your memory after a long period of looking.

Details You May Want to Consider

1. How do you like the neighborhood at different times of day?
2. Do you know what the traffic is like during rush hour?
3. How will the light be at different times of day? (Is the house too dark and dim, or too hot and bright?)
4. How does noise carry?
5. Does the floor plan "flow," or does it have a lot of tight corners and poorly placed appliances and cabinets?
6. Is the kitchen conveniently laid out?
7. Is there enough room for storage?
8. Will your favorite furniture fit, or are you willing to replace it?

You can also write your home notes on the back of the MLS information sheet that your agent will typically provide you for each property you visit. Then, when you get home, you can sit down and sift through your notes and start to rank the properties according to affordability, size, features, amenities, condition, layout, and location, among other things. After you do this a few times, it becomes easier to figure out which homes don't fit your needs and which ones do. Then, with a top ten list (or better yet, top two or three), you can ask your agent to take you back for a second look. Please note that in some markets and for some homes, you need to be prepared to move faster than the pace we are describing. You also may choose to check out some homes without your agent.

During your second visit to a home that has made the cut, take a little more time wandering through it and taking notes. Look a little more closely at the roof, walls, floors, layout, bedrooms, and bathrooms. Venture outside and stroll

around the yard, front and back. Imagine what it would be like to live th[...]
And then, when you think you've found the one, it's time to get serious
about making an offer, which we'll cover in the next chapter.

Notes to Take Home

- Careful consultation with your agent is the way to more
  accurately pinpoint what you are looking for. The right house
  will meet all your important needs, and as many of your
  additional wants as possible.

- The questions you should ask yourself include:
  1. What do I want my home to be close to?
  2. How much space do I need and why?
  3. Which is more critical: location or size?
  4. Would I be interested in a fixer-upper?
  5. How important is home value appreciation?
  6. Is neighborhood stability a priority?
  7. Would I be interested in a condo?
  8. Would I be interested in new home construction?
  9. What features and amenities do I want? Which do I really need?

- You'll learn as you look at homes—it's wise to refine your priorities along the way.

- Visit YourFirstHomeBook.com for worksheets and other helpful resources.

JAY'S FIRST HOME

When we lived in New York City, it never occurred to us to buy a home—almost everybody we knew rented. Then we moved to Austin, Texas, where I started working for Keller Williams. Mo Anderson, our CEO at the time, taught an orientation class on balance sheets, assets, and liabilities. She was passionate about building financial independence, and her advice sunk in. Suddenly, not buying a home just wasn't an option.

It didn't happen overnight. My wife Wendy and I spent a year paying off our college debt and saving money. But once we began looking, it happened really fast. People have always told me that when you find the right house you will know right away—kind of like meeting the right person and falling in love.

When we first saw the house pictured on the Internet, it didn't look at all promising. The black-and-white photograph, which had been taken through a metal chain-link fence in terrible lighting, made the house look dejected and sad. Still, it had the right address—in South Austin near Zilker Park and Barton Springs. It was the classic Austin neighborhood. And the price was right, too, only $5,000 more than we had budgeted.

The house looked even worse in person than in the photograph. Pink cinder block masquerading as stucco. No real driveway, just broken concrete and gravel. And, that ugly chain-link fence guarding an overgrown lawn. To make matters worse, it was raining that day. Then we opened the front door and went inside, and I remember saying to Wendy, "This is it."

That little bungalow had everything we valued: location, layout, and light. The previous owners had added a nice living space at the back with lots of windows. We immediately began referring to it as the sunroom.

Even though I knew this house was the one for us, we forced ourselves to look at four others that day. But by 9:45 in the evening we called our real estate agent and put in an offer. We bought it for $175,000.

My wife Wendy's dad is a great handyman, and she's pretty handy, too. He helped us install a new kitchen sink and garbage disposal. Wendy and I painted the house in bright pastel colors and put in a stone walkway and new floors. We ripped up the chain-link fence, except for the gate with the little metal lions on top, which became the focal point of our landscaping. My grandmother in Mississippi is known as "The Gardener." She gave us daylilies and hollyhocks to plant. Before long that little pink bungalow looked quite charming.

When I think of that first home, it reminds me of a carefree time with lots of dinner parties and hanging out with friends in the backyard. We have great memories of working on the improvements together. We spent three very happy years there until Gus, our first child, came along, and we needed to find something larger.

We still have that house and use it as rental property. Wendy enjoys showing it to prospective renters. She says it's easy to sell something you really love. The best part? That funny little house we bought for $175,000 appreciated to be worth more than $325,000 in only five years.

Although we didn't really plan it that way, it's turned out to be a great investment. As Wendy says, "It's the best investment we didn't know we were making."

Jay Papasan is vice president of publishing and executive editor of Keller Williams Realty International.

CHAPTER 5:
MAKE AN OFFER

• • • • •

Suzy Eskenazi, a buyer in Las Vegas, Nevada, lost the first house she put an offer on. There were forty competing offers, and hers simply wasn't the highest. It was all for the best, though, because a couple of weeks later Suzy walked into a home she liked even better. She wrote a deposit check on the spot. "People always say, 'You'll just know when you see it,'" she says. "It was true."

Suzy's story illustrates two general truths about shopping for homes. First, when you find a property that's right for you, most of the time you'll know it, so trust your instincts. Second, if that home doesn't work out, there will be another one. Every property search is different, but when you're standing in that home that just feels right, the time has come to write an offer.

> **The Three Components of an Offer**
>
> 1. Price
> 2. Terms
> 3. Contingencies

WRITING A STRONG OFFER

When you were searching for your dream home, you were just that—a dreamer. You needed to be romantic, to listen to your emotions, and to let yourself fall in love.

Now that you're writing an offer, we want you to remember you're a businessperson. You need to approach this process with a cool head and a realistic perspective on your market. The three basic components of an offer are price, terms, and contingencies (or "conditions" in Canada).

1) Price

One of the most common misconceptions buyers have about the home-buying process, agents agree, is thinking they're "supposed" to submit an offer that is below list price and then haggle to meet in the middle. In slow markets, this is a strategy that can work in your favor, but in fast ones, it can get you into trouble. Agent Jennifer Barnes once worked with a very successful young businessman who was determined to find "a deal." To him that meant paying well below list price. In his search to find a deal, though, he found a home he truly loved. He "lowballed" anyway, offering $120,000 under the $795,000 asking price. The sellers rejected his offer—and refused to deal with him again.

"That house was on the market for eight months, but they would not sell it to him," Jennifer says. "That's the risk you run when you lowball. You can personally affront the sellers so they just don't care that your money's green."

The right price fairly reflects the market value of the home you want to buy. To find this price, your agent will pull together a comparative market analysis (CMA), which is a set of MLS records about recently sold homes that resemble the one you want in size, condition, location, and amenities. These records are also called "comparables" or "comps." You'll get the best market insights from the homes most similar to your own. The perfect comp would be one that's identical to your dream home, situated next door, and that sold this morning. Perfect comps like that are hard to find, though, which is why writing a competitive offer is more of an art than a science.

WHAT'S A FAIR PRICE FOR 345 CARDINAL LANE?

Welcome to The Grasslands, a quiet neighborhood built in the 1960s. Most home here have three bedrooms, range from about 1,500 to 1,750 square feet, and have been selling between $140,000 and $180,000. You want to make an offer on 345 Cardinal Lane, listed at $165,000. What price will you offer?

 123 Eagle Pass

 345 Cardinal Lane

223 Robin Lane

- Three bedrooms
- 1.5 baths
- 1,550 square feet
- No recent updates
- On busy street
- Average-sized yard
- Listed as "handyman's special"

Sold last week for $90/square foot, or $139,500

- Three bedrooms
- Two baths
- 1,650 square feet
- Roof and kitchen both updated in the past five years
- Large yard
- On quiet street

You decide to offer $95/square foot, or $157,000

- Three bedrooms
- 2.5 baths
- 1,725 square feet
- Kitchen renovated last year
- Brand-new deck
- Huge backyard with landscaping
- On cul-de-sac
- Finished basement

Sold two weeks ago for $102/square foot, or $175,950

FIGURE 5.1

Your set of comps will enable you to determine an average cost per square foot, which forms the basis of a competitive offer. For example, imagine that on average, three-bedroom homes in Oak Knoll sold for about eighty-five dollars per square foot last month. The nicer homes sold for around ninety dollars per square foot, while those that needed a little work went for about eighty dollars. You need to decide where the home you want fits into that range. Does it need some updates? Is it located on one of the busier streets in the neighborhood? In that case, a fair price would probably be on the lower end. On the other hand, if it has an extra bathroom, a finished basement, or has been spectacularly maintained, you should probably offer a little more.

In either situation, remember we're talking above or below average, not necessarily above or below what the seller is asking. Smart sellers go through a similar process of comparison to price their homes fairly. If your math and the seller's figures work out the same, you may very well offer close to list price. But, if your analysis reveals that a property is indeed overpriced, go ahead and offer less. "Based on my agent Karoline Kelsen's market analysis, I offered somewhat below asking price. The seller countered somewhere in the middle, and we reached agreement. I followed my agent's lead because she does this for a living. You have to trust your agent," says Jeffrey Barg, a first-time home buyer.

However, be sure to factor in market realities. If you're facing a multiple-offer situation and you really love the property, you may decide to offer a little more than you would in a less-competitive market. A few thousand dollars may be a small price to pay to make sure your offer is accepted. "Sometimes people get so caught up in making a low offer they lose the house they really wanted," says agent Linda McKissack in Dallas, Texas. "I hate to see people so disappointed when $5,000 would have made all the difference."

Had Steve and Denise, from Austin, Texas, not acted decisively, such a multiple-offer scenario might have unfolded for them. They were engaged to be married and decided to buy a home Steve would move into before the wedding.

Their agent, Gary Keller, helped them create their home-hunting list. On a sheet of paper, Gary wrote "wants," and on the other side he wrote "needs." He then asked the couple to complete each list and to prioritize them.

As it turned out, there was one big problem. Given their wants and needs and their financial constraints, Gary could find only one home to show them. He just knew they'd love it. Sure enough, after walking through it, they looked like they were falling in love for "the second time." But then, Denise squeezed Steve's elbow and said, "And just think, this is the first one we've seen."

Gary sat with them on the couch right there in the living room, pulled out their wants and needs list, and asked them to review it. Steve and Denise had to agree the home was a match. They were just afraid things were happening too fast.

Gary explained that this was not only the perfect home for them, but actually the only home currently available. It had just come on the market, and they were the first to see it. He believed that the next people who saw the home would love it, too, and buy it. So, they had to be prepared to lose this home if they didn't buy it right then.

They agreed on a price, presented the offer, and the home was theirs. For years, Gary, Steve, and Denise reminisced about the experience. They were proud of their smart and courageous decision to buy it on the spot. And they agreed it wouldn't have been possible if Gary hadn't helped them be so clear about their priorities.

2) Terms

There's a lot more to real estate offers than price. You and the seller have to agree on many details, such as when the deal will close, whether the seller will keep any of the decor (such as window treatments or appliances), and who pays for closing costs. These factors are called terms, and they give buyers and sellers additional flexibility in crafting a win-win deal. When it comes to terms, we want you to remember that everything is negotiable. However, different markets have informal rules governing the kinds of requests you can make of sellers. Your agent will let you know what the seller will probably expect, as well as the pros and cons of deviating from market norms. The six basic terms in a real estate offer are schedule, conveyances, commission, closing costs, home warranty, and earnest money.

Schedule

As a first-time buyer, you have to fit closing day around moving, jobs, school, the end of your lease, and the expiration date on your loan preapproval. The seller has it even worse—simultaneously selling an old house and buying a new one. Your contract establishes a schedule for the events that have to happen before closing. If you write it well, it will keep things flowing smoothly for both you and the seller. In most contracts, the major milestones are:

- **Response time** (or "irrevocable time" in Canada). This is the period in which the seller must respond to your offer. It is usually no more than a few days.

- **Subject-to or contingency clauses** (or "conditions" in Canada). These are clauses that prevent a contract from becoming firm and binding and protect the buyer until the property is inspected, the title is searched, and financing is approved. The general clauses are the subject-to-inspection clause, the subject-to-marketable title clause, and the subject-to-financing clause. If the property inspection reveals that unsuspected, major repairs are needed or the title to the property is not clear (for example, if there are liens against the property) or if the buyer cannot obtain financing, then these clauses allow the buyer to walk away from the deal. These contingency clauses are discussed in more detail later in this chapter.

- **Expiration date** (or "requisition date" in Canada). This is the day before the deal must be closed. It's usually thirty to sixty days after the contract is accepted. If you or the seller don't have everything ready to close before the expiration date, it may be possible to extend the contract. However, neither of you has to accept the extension, so delays can kill the deal.

- **Occupancy date** (or "completion date" in Canada). This is the day you can move into your home. Generally, buyers want to take occupancy on closing day (or the next day, when the funds have officially cleared). Sellers, on the other hand, may often want the option of staying in the house after closing because it gives them more flexibility in arranging *their* home purchase. Because of liability issues, however, most agents recommend against allowing sellers to "lease back."

Should I Let the Seller Lease Back?

Sometimes sellers offer to pay rent on their house so they can stay in it after closing. This is called a "leaseback." Leasing back helps sellers coordinate moves or gives them certainty their old house is sold before they go under contract with the house they're buying. This kind of arrangement is risky for buyers, however. First of all, if the sellers damage anything after closing, you may have a hard time getting them to fix it. Plus, it exposes you to legal liability if they have an accident while living in the house that you now own. And, if the sellers delay in moving, you might even have to get involved in legal eviction proceedings.

Conveyances

Okay, so you're buying a home. What, exactly, is "a home"? No, this isn't one of those Zen questions to make you contemplate the nature of reality, such as "What is the sound of one hand clapping?" This is a question you need to spell out explicitly in your contract through a detailed list of conveyances.

Conveyances are the items that stay with the home when the sellers leave. In general, anything not permanently attached to the home is considered personal property, which goes with the seller, rather than "real property," or the fixtures, which stay. But what about those beautiful blinds that fit the picture window so perfectly? What about that expensive stainless steel fridge, or the antique chandelier in the dining room?

The standard contract forms used in your area may spell out which items typically convey in your area. And, the seller's disclosure oftentimes states what items the seller wants to keep. However, everything is negotiable. If you want something that isn't a wall, a roof, or a floor, and it's not already mentioned in the contract, you may want to add it to the forms. Sellers, however, can always say no—the trick is to negotiate, not make demands.

Commission

The real estate commission, or fee, for both the agent who works with the seller and the agent who works with the buyer in a transaction is usually paid for out of the sales price by the seller unless you, as the buyer, have arranged to pay the agent you work with separately. Please note that you can choose what is known as buyer representation and still have the fee come out of the transaction and paid by the seller.

Closing Costs

Buyers nearly always pay their own closing costs. However, if you're short on cash and want the seller to either pay closing costs outright (which is rare) or help you roll them into your loan (as explained in chapter 3), you need to write that into your contract.

Home Warranty

In many areas, it's common for sellers to provide a one-year home warranty. (In Canada sellers rarely provide a home warranty beyond closing date.) Home warranties are different from home owner's insurance, which can protect you from massive, unexpected tragedies like fires or break-ins. Warranties, on the other hand, cover repairs or replacement of appliances and major systems, such as the roof, plumbing, siding, or wiring. Read the warranty carefully to make sure that everything you want covered is included. If you wait until later to add new items, you'll probably have to get the home professionally inspected all over again, as warranty companies don't want you to wait for something to break before deciding to cover it.

Earnest Money

Earnest money, which is also called a deposit, protects the sellers from the possibility of you unexpectedly pulling out of the deal. If you're in a hot market, a large deposit can convince the sellers you're really serious about making the deal work. Earnest money is usually a percentage of the price of the property; it goes into an escrow account and becomes part of your down payment at closing. If the deal never reaches closing due to an error, omission, or decision on your part, you'll likely lose that money. (In Canada earnest money is deposited in a real estate trust account. Buyers who opt out of a deal may face greater liability than those in the United States. Check with your agent for details.)

3) Contingencies

Imagine you go under contract, and two days before closing, the seller leaves a candle burning and starts a fire that destroys half the house. Do you still want to buy the property according to the price and terms of your initial contract? Of course not. This is why most contracts include conditions or contingency clauses—they let you out of the deal if the house has a problem that didn't exist, or about which you weren't aware, when you went under contract. Again, standard contractual language varies from place to place, so when you're writing your contract, be sure to talk to your agent about which clauses are already included, and which you have to write in for yourself. There are five standard contingency clauses in a real estate contract: financing, inspections, clear title, condition at delivery, and community restrictions.

Financing

At its most basic, a financing contingency lets you out of the contract in the event that you can't qualify for a mortgage. In addition, it keeps you from being forced to accept an unfavorable mortgage if your loan paperwork comes in with a higher interest rate than you were promised. For example, a financing contingency might say that the contract is subject to your acquiring "a $150,000 mortgage for a term of thirty years at a rate of no higher than 7 percent." If the only loan you can find is at 10 percent, you can legally walk away from the contract.

Inspections

An inspection contingency protects you from paying too much for a home that's hiding major problems. For example, imagine you went under contract to buy 345 Grassy Knoll for $175,000, but a week later a property inspection (explained in chapter 6) revealed its sparkling appearance was hiding a failing foundation, out-of-date wiring, and nonfunctioning plumbing. Do you still want to pay $175,000? Do you even want to buy it at all? An inspection contingency enables you to renegotiate or walk away.

Clear Title

Just as some properties are hiding physical flaws, some homes are hiding legal flaws. A clear title contingency releases you from having to buy a home whose ownership is uncertain or that's subject to a lien to pay off the seller's debts.

Condition at Delivery

A good contract will require that the sellers leave the house vacant and in good condition. This prevents stressed-out sellers from leaving trash or old furniture they don't feel like moving. This is also what protects you in case something drastic happens to the home (such as a fire) before closing.

Community Restrictions

Many homes (particularly in new-home developments) reside in neighborhoods that require membership in a home owner's association. Consider including a contingency that lets you review and agree to the community covenants and restrictions and which will allow you to pull out of the deal if you don't like what you see—for example, the association fees are too high, or the neighborhood has rules you reject.

REACHING AGREEMENT

Once you and your agent have written a contract, your agent will submit it to the seller's agent. If you've written a great offer, the sellers might accept it on the spot. Otherwise, it's time to start negotiating. The sellers will write a counteroffer that, for example, asks for an earlier closing date and a slightly higher price. Then the ball is back in your court to decide whether to accept their changes or whether to counter their counter.

If the idea of negotiating makes you nervous, don't worry—you won't negotiate directly with the seller. Instead, your agent will do all the talking with the seller's agent, providing a buffer between you and the seller and saving you the stress of in-person negotiations. Remember, negotiating skills were one of the main qualities you looked for when you hired your agent, and this is when the great ones get another chance to excel.

Amy Sue Graham of Exton, Pennsylvania, secured the purchase of her home in large part due to the thoughtful efforts of her agent Matt Fetick. Matt wrote a letter and sent it to the sellers with the Graham's offer. He thought that telling their story—the fact they spent their first year of married life apart because Amy's husband had been deployed to Iraq—would add personal meaning to their purchase offer. "We were competing against other offers, one of which was $10,000 more than ours. Later, the seller's agent told me the letter helped us get that home," says Amy.

When you and the seller reach agreement and both parties sign the contract, that check you wrote as earnest money will be deposited into an escrow account (or in a real estate trust account in Canada). An escrow agent is a neutral third party, often a title company or specialized escrow company (the specifics vary from province to province and state to state) that holds the deposit until closing day. This is called "opening escrow" or "going under contract." (In Canada the listing broker, who holds the funds in a trust, typically fulfills the same duties as the escrow agent.) When that happens, you've passed another major, exciting milestone. The last task awaiting you before closing? To remove all the contingencies standing between you and a closed deal, which you'll get to learn about in the next chapter.

Notes to Take Home

- You now know and understand the three basic components of a purchase offer: price, terms, and contingencies.

- Price—the right price to offer must fairly reflect the true market value of the home you want to buy. Your agent's market research will guide this decision.

- Terms—the other financial and timing factors that will be included in the offer. Terms fall under six basic categories in a real estate offer: Follow these six steps to financing your home:

    1. Schedule—a schedule of events that has to happen before closing.

    2. Conveyances—the items that stay with the house when the sellers leave.

    3. Commission—the real estate commission or fee, for both the agent who works with the seller and the agent who works with the buyer.

    4. Closing costs—it's standard for buyers to pay for their closing costs, but if you want to roll the costs into the loan, you need to write that into the contract.

    5. Home warranty—this covers repairs or replacement of appliances and major systems, such as the roof, plumbing, siding, or wiring. You may ask the seller to pay for this.

    6. Earnest money—this protects the sellers from the possibility of your unexpectedly pulling out of the deal. It makes a statement about the seriousness of your offer.

- Contingencies (or "conditions")—these clauses let you out of the deal if the house has a problem that didn't exist, or about which you weren't aware, when you went under contract. They specify any even that will need to take place in order for you to fulfill the contract.

- Visit YourFirstHomeBook.com for worksheets and other helpful resources.

MARK'S FIRST HOME

I grew up in Houston, Texas, with a rising real estate market driven by a booming energy industry. By the time I was sixteen, my parents had bought and sold some six houses. Each sale brought a move for the family and financial reward to my parents. Over time I watched some of the houses they purchased nearly double in value. I knew they were on to something, and I recognized that buying a home is the single most important and safest investment you can make in your life. It was important for me to participate in the experience as fast as I could.

As a business major in college, I thought about my first home purchase strictly as an investment. I knew that I could find a place that would not cost much more than what I was paying in rent, so buying a home made perfect sense. I also knew I would not be living in the place forever, so I saw it as a launching pad from which I could embark on my own journey of home ownership.

Fortunately, I got my chance during my junior year in college. I found a property on the north side of town in Austin, Texas—a wonderful new condominium development in a great location—and pulled together the deal. My mother generously gifted the down payment and cosigned. After living in dorms and campus housing, I felt elated about moving into a brand new place. Most of all, I liked the opportunity to stop paying rent and start building equity.

My new home began as a bachelor pad. I moved into it with a roommate whose rent payments helped offset my mortgage. At only 900 square feet the place was small, but it had a smart, two-level floor plan with two bedrooms upstairs and many attractive amenities throughout. It was a place where my friends would gather for poker games, pool parties, and barbecues on the patio beneath a beautiful oak tree. The location was near perfect, within walking distance of the grocery store, a nearby restaurant, and even the university.

I lived there while I finished college, worked, and got married. My wife, Cindy, and I happily spent our first year of married life there, and we have many fond memories. One was the night Cindy and I got engaged. We arrived home to a surprise party thrown by our friends. Another memory was the day my wife and I returned home from our honeymoon. She asked me to step out for a few hours. So I did. And when I returned, I found the decor distinctly different. Gone were many of the trappings of bachelorhood, replaced by a pink and blue bedspread, and many of the warm touches that only Cindy could provide. One of my most distinct memories is of the time Cindy and I went walking in five inches of snow—a true Texas rarity.

In the year we lived there together, my wife and I made several improvements. Since we wanted to sell, we had to distinguish it from other units in the complex. So, in a few months' time, we repainted the walls, added crown molding, and installed hardwood floors. Our upgrade efforts really transformed the home. Not only did we make it more comfortable for ourselves, but we also increased its value and appeal to prospective buyers. Eventually, when the time came to sell, we found a buyer and walked away $15,000 richer.

Our first experience was so positive that it became the model for every home purchase since. My wife and I have bought five other homes together. Each time, we bought the first or second property we saw. That confidence began with the purchase of our first home and it has carried on throughout our life together. Cindy and I both learned that when you buy your very first home you have fundamentally made a commitment to larger possibilities in your life.

Mark Willis served as chief executive officer of Keller Williams Realty, Inc., from 2005 to 2015.

CHAPTER 6:
PERFORM DUE DILIGENCE

· · · · ·

Tonja Pitzer of Tulsa, Oklahoma, fell in love with a 1920s home with a big, beautiful front porch. She quickly put it under contract and ordered her inspection. The report, however, wasn't pretty. There were termite problems. Gutters were falling down. The garage was keeling over. The entire home had antiquated knob-and-tube wiring. And, she discovered, the porch provided an even bigger surprise.

"There were only a few bricks holding it up," she says. "The ground underneath the porch was wearing away, so every few years the owners would stuff another brick underneath the post to hold it up."

Rather than negotiating extensive repairs, Pitzer decided to walk away.

"I loved that house and hated to let it go," she says. "But with all those problems, it didn't make sense to buy it."

If you get to the point where it's better to walk away, we don't want you to make the mistake some buyers make—worry that the money they spent on the inspection is "wasted."

"The $400 you spend inspecting a house you don't buy may be the best $400 you've ever spent," says Kansas City, Missouri, agent Steve Johns. "It saves you from buying a disaster."

Unlike most major purchases, once you buy a home, you can't return it if something breaks or doesn't quite work like it's supposed to. That's why home owner's insurance and property inspections are so important. The property inspection should expose all the secret issues a home can hide—such as a leaking pipe under the bathroom sink, a rusted hot water heater, or lead-based paint on bedroom walls—so you know exactly what you are getting into when you sign the closing papers. And if something breaks after you move in, you also want to make sure you have purchased sufficient property insurance to cover any major damage.

When you wrote your contract, you assumed certain things about the home you want to buy. The property inspection and insurability check may produce a new sense of confidence in the home you're buying, or they might kick off another round of negotiations with the sellers. In the worst-case scenario, the inspection and check may cause you to walk away from the deal. No matter what happens, you'll know you took all the right steps to make sure your home purchase was a sound investment and didn't put you at unexpected risk. "The home inspection really protects the buyer. It doesn't remove risk from the purchase, but it does reduce the risk. Think of it as a bill of health on the home you're buying," says agent Bruce Hardie of Spokane, Washington.

GET A HOME OWNER'S INSURANCE POLICY

Having a home owner's insurance policy is smart. It's also usually necessary—you can't get a mortgage without one. However, getting a policy on an older home can sometimes be complicated. Many insurance companies now require upgrades, renovations, and retrofitting—such as replacing outdated wiring—before they will issue a policy. So, we want to encourage you to act quickly so you can find out what you need to update, as well as negotiate repairs with the seller, get them done, and have a policy in hand on closing day. "I've never had a house that couldn't get insured, but I have seen situations where companies demanded proof that repairs were made right down to the close of escrow," says California agent Karen Halladay.

To choose a policy, we recommend you start by calling a few companies referred by trusted and knowledgeable sources, including your real estate agent. Once they give you quotes, you can compare policies and premiums. Policies vary dramatically, so put in the time to choose the right one.

Choosing a Policy

A basic home owner's insurance policy protects you in two ways. First, it insures against loss or damage to the property itself, such as a fire or hail damage. Second, it also protects against liability in case someone sustains an injury while on your property, such as by slipping on ice in your driveway. However, there are many ways you can add to or amend basic policies. Most insurance companies also offer varying deductible rates, which can impact your annual premium (i.e., the higher the deductible, the lower the premium). We believe the following questions will help you sort through your many options:

How much coverage do you need?

You don't have to buy insurance for the entire purchase price of your home. That price includes the cost of the land beneath it, which is virtually impossible to ruin and which doesn't need to be insured. So, your $150,000 home may need only a $130,000 policy if the land beneath it is worth $20,000.

Replacement cost or actual cash value?

One of the most important choices is whether you want to insure your home for replacement cost or actual cash value. Actual cash value is the price of the home: if the home you insure today for $150,000 burns down ten years from now, you will be given $150,000 with which to replace it. Unfortunately for actual-cash-value policyholders, increasing construction costs means that $150,000 will buy less and less home as the years go by. That's why most buyers choose a replacement-cost policy, which is a little more expensive, but will pay for rebuilding your home, no matter the cost.

What are the named and unnamed perils?

Home damage can come in many forms, from the predictable, such as fires or break-ins, to the bizarre (meteorites, runaway trucks, escaped circus animals). The best policy is all-peril: It covers damage from anything not specifically excluded in the policy language. It's a little more expensive, but it protects against surprises. A named-peril policy covers only damage that is specifically listed in the policy. If you accept the risk of a named-peril policy, be sure you understand exactly what the policy does and doesn't cover.

Do you need personal property insurance?

If your home is damaged or destroyed, it's unlikely that your possessions would survive unscathed. Once you add up what it would cost to replace all your possessions, from your socks to your dishes to your furniture, it's obvious why so many buyers add personal property insurance to their policies. If you own extremely valuable or one-of-a-kind possessions, such as fine jewelry or art, we want you to know you can purchase additional coverage on top of the standard ratio. Be sure you check whether a personal property policy will cover your possessions no matter where the loss or damage occurs. If your laptop is stolen when you're on vacation, for example, this kind of policy can be beneficial.

What are your additional living expenses?

This covers your costs if, for example, you're stuck in a hotel for a month while damage to your home is repaired.

Specialized Insurance

Your standard policy most likely won't cover damage from geographically predictable perils, such as hurricanes in Florida or earthquakes in California. If you live on a coast or near a fault line, you may want to consider purchasing extra protection. In fact, it may be required—lenders in flood-prone areas, for example, often require buyers to purchase flood insurance as a condition for approving the mortgage.

Proof and Prepayment

Once you choose a policy, your company will send proof of insurance to your lender that officially clears one of the hurdles on your road to closing. The insurance company will also make arrangements for you to prepay a year's worth of premiums as part of your closing costs.

PROPERTY INSPECTION

At the same time that you're shopping for insurance, you should also shop for a property inspector. A home includes dozens of systems and features, all of which make our lives comfortable and pleasant, but all of which can cause serious headaches (and wallet-aches) when they malfunction. If you buy a new blender and it doesn't work, you can take it back to the store. If you buy a new property and discover on the first rainy day that the roof leaks, unfortunately you're now the proud owner of a leaky roof. An inspection exposes your dream home's hidden flaws, so you can go back to the seller to negotiate before you become the owner. Typically, sellers will either agree to fix the problems or reduce the sales price to cover your cost of fixing them. However, if an owner is selling a home "as-is," the seller may refuse to do either. In that case, you'll have to decide if you're willing to buy the home at the previously agreed-to price, glitches and all.

Before you hire your own inspector, we encourage you to carefully review the seller's disclosure, a written statement of the owners' knowledge of the property's current condition. (Your agent will get the disclosure from the seller's agent.) For example, you may be considering a property that another buyer previously had under contract, but who had pulled out when the buyer's inspector found a major crack in the foundation. The seller would have to include that information in the disclosure, giving you the opportunity to walk away (if you wanted to) before springing for another inspection.

Finding an Inspector

The information your inspector provides will be critical to your making a well-informed home-buying decision. In other words, this is no time to scan the Yellow Pages. As always when you're hiring a professional, start by collecting referrals from people you trust. If you want to interview a few candidates, the following questions will help:

Are you licensed, or a member of a professional inspector's organization?

Inspectors are required to be licensed in about a dozen states (your agent can tell you if they are in yours). In U.S. states where licenses aren't required, membership in a professional organization, such as the American Society of Home Inspectors (ASHI), is a good sign. In Canada you'll want to look for professionals who are members of the Canadian Association of Home and Property Inspectors® (CAHPI®).

What is your professional background?

A background in a highly skilled profession, such as engineering, can come in handy.

What kind of ongoing training do you receive?

Building techniques and codes change over time, so even good inspectors need a refresher.

Do you have errors and omission insurance?

This protects inspectors—and you—if they make a mistake that leads you to buy a flawed home.

Can I see a sample inspection report?

Look for detailed descriptions of the strengths and possible flaws in each of the home's systems, not just a checklist of whether they're working.

Do you specialize in a certain kind of construction?

Properties often have quirks related to their age, location, or construction style. Working in Long Beach, California, agent Shannon Jones says she sees many homes with foundation troubles because of the particular kind of beach sand used in their construction. So, when one of her clients is considering a home with that sort of foundation, she steers the person toward an expert who knows exactly what to inspect. Brand-new homes also have quirks that call for a specialist. We don't want you to be unduly stressed; your agent can help you decide whether your home needs a specialized inspector.

What does it cost?

Inspections can cost as little as $200 or more than $1,000, and you'll be responsible for that cost whether you buy the property or not. The price is determined by several factors. First, some inspectors charge more—a higher price may indicate higher quality. In addition, larger homes and those with more bathrooms and air-conditioning units cost more because they require more work. However, Debbie Abadie, a Houston, Texas, agent who is also a licensed inspector, warns buyers to avoid inspectors who base their quotes on the price of the home. It takes about the same amount of work to inspect a 2,000-square-foot home with two bathrooms, whether the sales price is $100,000 or half a million. "If the inspector asks how much you're paying for the house, hang up as fast as you can," she adds.

How soon are you available?

Because the results of an inspection may launch you into negotiations and repairs that must be completed before closing, it's important to schedule an inspection (at a time you can attend) as quickly as possible.

New Houses Need Inspection, Too

We recommend you don't neglect the inspection just because you're buying a brand-new home. In fact, flaws in new construction can be even harder to spot than in older homes because their symptoms haven't had a chance to show up yet. Buyer Teresa Van Horn, for example, didn't discover for months that a slow leak from an improperly welded pipe was rotting out the bathroom wall of her new condo. When her newly completed condo was inspected, the pipe was already hidden behind the pristine, white wall.

If you're buying a new home, definitely find an inspector who specializes in new construction. Agent Amy Denham in Florida suggests buyers go one step further. "If they can handle the additional expense, I recommend that my buyers have the builder's work inspected during the construction on a periodic basis," she says. "That way, if a mistake is made, you can catch it before it's too far along."

WHAT TO EXPECT WHEN YOU'RE INSPECTING

No matter how busy you are, you should attend your inspection. It's your big chance to get a professional introduction to the fuse box, air-conditioning system, water heater, and other systems you may soon own.

Plus, inspectors aren't required to move furniture or look under carpets, so it's possible for even good inspectors to miss things. Asheville, North Carolina, agent Tony Marin attended an inspection where the basement walls were lined with plastic. When he peeled away a corner of the plastic, Marin found it was covering a major crack in the foundation. "That's the kind of thing that's typical for an inspector to miss," he says.

IN YOUR INSPECTION: IT'S THE BIG STUFF THAT REALLY MATTERS

While small repairs can add up, your major concern is structural damage. This can come from water damage, shifting ground, or poor construction when the house was built.

THE BIG STUFF

1. Major cracks or crumbling in foundation. (Hairline cracks are usually OK.)
2. Jagged or diagonal cracks inside the house, especially over the windows or doors.
3. Water stains in ceilings, floors, or walls.
4. Faded, worn shingles may mean the roof needs replacing. If the shingles are damaged, it's possible the decking underneath is too.
5. Stains on the basement walls (or brand-new paint that may be covering stains) suggest water damage that can cause mold or structural problems. At the very least, it suggests a persistently leaky basement.

"So that's why you have to go along, and you really have to look."

While you probably don't want to move furniture around to see what sellers are hiding—imagine the liability if you knocked over the entertainment center in your quest to look behind it!—you can certainly flip back the throw rug to see if it's covering cracked tiles. And in the end, an extra set of eyes can only help.

REPAIRS AND RENEGOTIATION

Once you have your inspection report, we want you to know your first job is simple: *read it*.

Many agents say they're amazed by the number of people who approach their inspection like a hurdle to jump over, rather than as a valuable new source of information about the property they're considering to buy.

"When my daughter bought her house, she didn't pay attention to the details of her inspection and ended up with all sorts of problems," says one New York agent. "This is all too common. In the rush of things, people don't take time to read the report and miss the opportunity to make the seller take care of problems for them."

So you're flipping through your inspection report, noting page after page of problems the inspector found in your "former" dream home. Your first response, when you get to page five or so, is probably a heartfelt "Eeeeek!"

Don't panic. There are no perfect homes. Unless your home is new, it's virtually guaranteed to have some wear and tear. An inspector's job is to note everything—everything—that's not perfect about the property, right down to the minor, easily fixed "problems," such as replacing missing window screens or broken switch plates, which annoy just about everyone. However, asking a seller to repair every loose doorknob is a surefire deal-killer. Custom (not to mention common sense) dictates that buyers not ask the unreasonable. But what, exactly, is "unreasonable"? This will vary from place to place and market to market, and your real estate agent will be able to guide you toward what is and isn't a typical, reasonable request.

"Put yourself in the seller's shoes," says agent Shannon Jones. "If there are any health-and-safety concerns, most people would consider those repairs reasonable. But most sellers will say no if you just come in with a laundry list." In short, the right way to handle your inspection report is to avoid demanding the sellers fix every little thing. Instead, take the time to sort out problems that are actually worth worrying about and negotiating over.

Deciding Which Repairs Matter

There are certain problems buyers typically ask sellers to handle. These include deferred maintenance, such as cleaning the pool or gutters, or having a neglected heating or air-conditioning system serviced. As always, local norms help provide a guide. "We have many septic systems and wells, and sellers typically pay for their septic systems to be pumped and inspected," says agent Roy Van Winkle. "That's not written anywhere, but it's just expected."

The kinds of problems you encounter will depend on your region. Shifting foundations and termites are common in the South; basement leaks or insulation problems frequently occur up North. Your agent will be able to estimate what many common repairs will cost; in some cases he or she may recommend calling in a contractor for an estimate. Once you see your repair bill, you can decide what to ask the seller to fix, and what you're comfortable repairing (either with or without a repair allowance).

We suggest you exercise caution when deciding how to handle problems—such as leaks, electrical work, or pests—that require opening walls. It can often be difficult to tell how extensive such problems are from the outside, so when you open the wall, you may find a much larger problem than you bargained for. So, ask the sellers to handle inside-the-wall repairs, if possible. Otherwise, you may negotiate a repair allowance of one amount, only to find once the drywall is in pieces that fixing the problem will cost five times more than you expected.

If you're thinking of taking on a major repair, we encourage you to factor in your short- and long-term plans. If you're staying only a few years, extensive repairs may not be worth the hassle. On the other hand, if this is the home you intend to live in for many years, it can be exciting to take the reins on an upgrade that will last a lifetime.

REACHING FINAL AGREEMENT

Once you've decided what you need to have fixed in order to make the purchase, your agent will convey your requests to the sellers. We want you to remember your options include asking the seller to make repairs or asking for compensation (either through reducing the sales price or through a cash repair allowance) so you can make them yourself. And, if there isn't much wrong with the home, the simplest option is to move forward with the original contract without asking the sellers to fix anything.

Once you get to the point of negotiating repairs, everyone is usually a little tense. You're so close to having a deal! Still, all the emotions and excitement you and the seller feel can needlessly blow relatively minor issues —such as who will pay for the new $300 water heater in your $200,000 home—out of proportion. This is dangerous because the seller could reject your counter and kill the deal if it starts to seem like it will be easier to find another buyer than to find agreement. Good negotiating, then, means having a clear understanding of where you're willing to give as well as what matters most and communicating those priorities to the sellers. If negotiations prove difficult, you could decide you love the home enough to buy it, flaws and all. As a very last resort, the inspection contingency will let you walk away.

There's a good chance you and the seller eventually will reach agreement. At that point, you'll have a finalized contract and a home owner's insurance policy (or at least you'll be well on your way to getting one). These two steps are probably the last big hurdles you'll have to face. We've finally arrived at an exciting moment: the time it becomes fairly certain that this home really will be yours. The last few steps between here and closing, which include a survey, title work, and appraisal, are handled primarily by your agent and lender and are explained in the next chapter.

Notes to Take Home

- A home owner's insurance policy protects you in two ways:

  1. Against loss or damage to the property itself
  2. Against liability in case someone sustains an injury while on your property.

- The property inspection (which we highly recommend you attend) should expose all the secret issues a home might hide. So you know exactly what you are getting into before you sign closing papers keep the following in mind:

  1. Your main concern is the possibility of structural damage. This can come from water damage, shifting ground, or poor construction when the house was built.
  2. Don't sweat the small stuff. It's the inspector's job to mark everything discovered no matter how large or small. Things that are easily fixed can be overlooked.
  3. If you have a big problem show up in your inspection report, you should bring in a specialist and if the worst-case scenario turns out to be true, you might want to walk away from the purchase.

DIANNA'S FIRST HOME

Responsibility came naturally to me very early. I started working in my parents' grocery store at the age of five. When my brother became ill and had to leave town for treatment, my parents, who accompanied him, actually left Lila, my coworker, and me in charge of the store. I was only in the eighth grade. So, by the time I was nineteen, it seemed perfectly normal and sensible to be buying my first house.

At that time, I lived in Arvada, Colorado, a suburb of Denver, and everything the real estate agents showed me in my price range needed fixing up. Finally, another agent told me about a small group of newly built homes. I bought one for $19,500. That was in 1970.

My parents had rented for a long time before buying their first home. While I lived with them, we couldn't even hang a picture on the wall because our houses belonged to someone else. Now that I had my own home, I got a chance to choose my own finishes and fixtures!

My husband and I sold that first house one year later for around $25,000, and we poured the money we had in savings into buying what I truly consider to be my first home. Before making this purchase, we armed ourselves with a list of "must-haves." It must have a huge yard and a playroom for our future children and their friends. It must have a two-car garage so we wouldn't have to scrape ice from the cars in order to open their doors after a winter storm. It must have a large kitchen where I could do a lot of baking. And it must have a big enough family room for large gatherings.

It took awhile, but we absolutely found the house that fit our "must-haves" with only one exception: it wasn't located on a beach or lake, as I'd always imagined my dream house would be. This house had a big kitchen that overlooked the family room and a second family room downstairs that had been soundproofed. It had belonged to one of the members of the Nitty Gritty Dirt Band—our big claim to fame.

You accumulate so many memories when you live in a home for twenty-four years. I remember my two boys learning to ride their bikes in the driveway, our hosting their birthday parties, and people dropping by all the time. Our house was known in the neighborhood as the gingerbread house because each

Christmas I'd bake gingerbread and we would invite the kids over to build houses out of the pieces of bread.

Each week, we designated one special night as family night. The kitchen and dining area had a step up from the family room, and if you used your imagination it could pass for a stage. We'd push back the furniture, and the kids would put on a show. We loved that night.

Life is all about progress. My sons are grown now and do a lot of public speaking—I guess it's still showtime. I'm living in Austin, Texas, and loving my Keller Williams career. And what about my dream home on the water? I now have three!

Dianna Kokoszka is CEO of KW MAPS Coaching at Keller Williams Realty International.

CHAPTER 7:
CLOSE

· · · · ·

The week before closing was an emotional one for Becky Pastner of Austin, Texas. She was crazy about the adorable bungalow she had found and thrilled at the prospect of becoming a home owner at the age of twenty-six. Still, she found herself in tears the night before closing. "Of course I was happy to be buying a home," Becky recalls, "but I was just so full of emotions."

She was still tense and jittery the next morning as she and her husband drove to their lender's office in a downpour. They were so nervous they got lost on the way. Everything changed, however, the moment they sat down at the closing table. "As soon as we got inside, I knew everything was going to be OK," says Becky. The storm even blew over while they were signing their paperwork, so when Becky stepped outside, the bright sunshine seemed to reflect perfectly the elation of finally owning her own home. As your closing day approaches, you might be feeling pretty emotional, too. That's normal—just remind yourself that you're in the homestretch.

Preclosing Verifications

1. Stay in control of your finances.
2. Return all phone calls and paperwork promptly.
3. Communicate with your agent at least once a week.
4. Several days before closing, confirm with your agent that all your documentation is in place and in order.
5. Obtain certified funds for closing.
6. Conduct a final walk-through.

The final stage is the lender's confirmation of the home's value and legal status, and your continued credit-worthiness. This entails a survey, appraisal, title search, and a final check of your credit and finances. Your agent will keep you posted on how each is progressing, but unlike the previous stages, your work is pretty much done. At this point, you don't have much to worry about other than keeping your finances tight and your credit clean and confirming with your agent that you'll have all the necessary documents and funds you'll need so you can move smoothly into your closing day—and into your new life as a home owner.

FINAL VERIFICATIONS

Just as you confirmed the value of the home you're buying through a property inspection, lending institutions also take certain steps before finalizing a mortgage to make sure they are backing a sound investment. These include:

- An appraisal to confirm the value of the property
- A survey to confirm the legal boundaries and entitlements of the property
- A title search to verify the ownership of the property
- Title insurance to protect against mistakes in the title search

Chances are good that these final steps—which, incidentally, you will pay for as part of your closing costs—will go smoothly. We want you to remember that the whole point of these preclosing verifications is to look for problems that occasionally arise. If you run into a patch of trouble, think of it this way: it's better for a title search or survey to reveal a property's questionable ownership or boundaries before closing, rather than after the house is already yours.

Appraisal

Imagine a buyer takes out a $150,000 loan on a home and promptly defaults. If your lending institution can't resell that house for $150,000, it loses money. To protect against that possibility, your lender will require an independent appraisal of your home's value before finalizing your mortgage. Appraisers do exactly what you and your agent did when you were deciding how much to offer for your home: compare the property you're buying to others in the area in terms of size, condition, location, and amenities. In most cases, appraisers generate a reasonable fair market value, one which falls in the same range that buyers discover.

Every once in a while, though, appraisers think homes are worth less than what the buyer and seller have agreed to. This can happen for several reasons. Perhaps the seller made improvements without getting necessary permits, so appraisers can't legally count them in the home's value. Or, buyers in fast-moving markets offer more than the asking price to make sure their offer is accepted.

Your lender won't write a loan for more than a home's appraised value, so if your appraisal comes in low, you'll have to figure out a way to cover the gap. For example, let's say you're under contract for a $200,000 home, and you planned to put $40,000 down and borrow $160,000. If the property appraises for less and the lender will only lend you $150,000, you will have to come up with the shortfall and pay an additional $10,000 down to close. In situations like these, sometimes the seller lowers the price, sometimes the buyer pays the extra cash, or sometimes the buyer and seller split the difference. You can also dispute the appraisal and ask the lender to order a new one—this is definitely worth a shot if you think the appraiser misjudged a fast-moving market. But if all else fails, we want you to know you can exercise the financing contingency in your contract and walk away. (Conditions often have expiration dates in Canada. Be sure to find out what you need to know about your home, such as the appraisal, before any financing condition expires.)

Survey

When subdivisions are new, it's obvious where one yard stops and another begins. As the years pass, however, and people build fences, sheds, and additions, it's common for the boundaries to blur. That's why a survey is needed. It provides a bird's-eye view of the property lines to make sure your new home (and garage, shed, fence, and other structures) doesn't touch someone else's property. It also confirms the location of easements, areas upon which property owners aren't supposed to build. The most common are utility easements that allow government entities permanent access to power and sewer lines. That access includes the right to tear down anything within the easement that would keep these entities from working. It may seem amazing that people would build their new dining room within an easement, but every agent has a story about the long-time home owner who forgot to check for easements when a pool, addition, or detached garage was built.

We know surveys can also protect you from downright fraudulent sales. Agent Carol Peyton of Houston, Texas, knew home owners who were buying a property and who bought what they thought was one huge parcel of land. They were wrong. "When they went to see the property, the owner pointed to the land and obliquely said, 'There it is,'" Carol explained. "They thought they were buying the whole thing, but it was actually two separate tracts of land, and they were only buying half of it."

If a seller has a recent survey, lenders will usually accept it. However, if the survey is more than a few years old, lenders usually require a new one. Typically, the lender commissions the survey, and you pay for it as part of your closing costs. You keep the survey at closing, so make sure you store it in a safe place. That way, when you decide to build an addition, you'll know where not to put the new dining room!

Title

It's surprising enough that home owners sometimes forget the precise locations of their property lines. More shocking is the kind of confusion that can arise over who has legal ownership, or "title," to a piece of property. Factors such as divorce, death, and debts can create legal conundrums over who has the right to call a house, "my home."

"I've seen just about everything," says loan officer Larry Weisinger of Austin, Texas. "It can be nuts." He's seen closings get held up when the home being sold belonged to a home owner who died without a will, forcing the title company to track down every potential heir to approve the deal before it could close. His own grandmother faced a typically bizarre title problem due to a thirty-year-old divorce. In 1967, she married a divorced man and moved into the home he had owned with his previous wife. She lived in the home for three decades, even though technically the ex-wife legally owned half of it. When the ex-wife died, however, her two children showed up seeking "their" half of the property.

These sorts of problems are why lenders require a title search and title insurance before closing. Getting a title search is like getting screened for rare diseases in your annual checkup: there probably won't be a problem, but if there is, you need to know about it right away. A title company (or in Canada a real estate lawyer) protects your deal by researching the title for liens, encumbrances (claims against property), and other so-called "clouds." In addition to disputed ownership, title searches protect you from unpaid liens, which are claims against the seller's debts. For example, you don't want to buy a home from someone in a dispute with the IRS over unpaid taxes—if the IRS (or its equivalent, Canada Revenue Agency) goes after the property, you could get caught in the middle.

Even with all that searching, title companies sometimes miss things. That's why your lender will also require you to buy title insurance that covers your costs if, for example, the missing heir does show up a few years down the road. Title insurance also covers mistakes in survey interpretation. For example, agent Andra Morris of Austin, Texas, wanted to buy a home with a lovely pool in the backyard. When the seller had bought the property, however, he hadn't noticed a utility easement in the same place as the pool, and neither had his title company. Andra bought the home, but she made sure to get her title insurance through the company that made the initial mistake. That way, if the water department showed up one day to tear up her pool, the insurance would pay for its replacement.

KEEP YOURSELF "MORTGAGE WORTHY"

You may be a minor player in the appraisal and title work, but when it comes to finalizing the loan, you're still the star. That's because your lender will check your finances just before closing to make sure you're in the same good financial shape you were in when the lender preapproved you a month or two ago. Your job is to remain that credit-worthy person: keep your discretionary spending to a minimum, don't buy anything on credit, and whatever you do, don't spend your cash reserves.

Unfortunately, every agent has a story about buyers who didn't realize they needed to keep their financial profiles spotless right up until closing. In their excitement to settle into their beautiful new homes, some buyers jump the gun on buying furniture and appliances. Then, when the lender pulls their credit, they find that their scores have dropped, sometimes so much that they no longer qualify for a loan.

"I worked with a couple who bought a truckload of furniture on credit just before closing," says agent Don Beach in Tulsa, Oklahoma. "They had marginal credit to begin with, and those purchases pushed them out of the acceptable range. We found out the night before closing." Fortunately, Don was able to strike an agreement with the furniture company to "return" the furniture until the deal was closed. The move restored the couple's credit, so despite a few frantic, stressful hours, they ended up with both the home and the furniture.

That's not the only way buyers jeopardize their transactions. Some carelessly spend their down payment or the money they had put away for closing costs. This can lead to some frantic maneuvers to find cash at the last minute. "I had a buyer who day-traded to come up with his down payment," says agent Dave Tower in Florida. "The buyer literally said, 'I bought 3,000 shares this morning and I'm hoping they'll go up a dollar and a half by noon.' We closed, but it was nerve-racking."

We want you to spare yourself the tension: go into a financial deep-freeze as soon as you start home shopping. Don't make any major purchases and keep your minor spending in check. After all, you'll be able to make extra spending decisions once you officially own your home.

COUNTDOWN TO CLOSING

Once you and the home have checked out, you'll receive your final loan commitment. Only then will the closing company schedule a time and place for the closing. (In Canada you should discuss the schedule of the closing with your lawyer.) As the big day approaches, confirm with your agent (or in Canada, your lawyer) that you have everything you need in order to close and transition smoothly into your new home. This will include the following:

- Settlement statement (or "Statement of Adjustments" in Canada)
- Certified funds
- Evidence of insurance

Settlement Statement

The settlement statement is a final, official rendering of the terms of your loan and your exact closing costs. It's sometimes called a HUD statement (or "Statement of Mortgage" in Canada), and by law, your lender must provide it at least a day before closing. Requesting it sooner, however, gives you more time to compare it with your good-faith estimate. If your interest rate or any fees are higher than what you were promised, we advise you to call your agent immediately. This is also a good time to have your agent explain any fees you still don't understand so you won't feel perplexed on closing day.

Certified Funds

When you're buying a property, you can't just whip out your checkbook at the closing table. You will need to pay your down payment and closing costs with certified funds from a financial institution. Once you have a settlement statement, you can go to your bank and get the precise amount of funds you'll need in the form of a cashier's check or by having your bank wire that amount to your closing escrow account.

Evidence of Insurance

Your lender will need proof that you really have secured your home owner's insurance, which comes in the form of an "evidence of insurance" letter from your company. Don't forget: part of that evidence is prepaying a year's worth of insurance premiums.

Transfer of Utilities

You're no doubt looking forward to the first candlelit dinner in your new home. However, candles will be your only option if you forgot to transfer the utilities into your name and have no electricity. A couple of weeks before closing, you should contact all the appropriate utility and service providers (gas, electricity, water, garbage, telephone, cable, among others) to arrange for transfer of services on your tentative closing date. Typically, most service companies will allow for an overlap so service remains intact during a move-out and move-in.

Movers

Many agents recommend hiring movers as a way to minimize hassle. However, the decision of whether to use them is a personal one that encompasses how much cash you have after your home purchase, as well as how you feel about strangers packing your stuff. If you plan to use movers, schedule them as soon as possible (a month out would not be too soon). And, you should hire a moving company the same way you hire any other professional: by collecting referrals from satisfied customers. After all, some of the most irreplaceable things in our homes have virtually no financial value against which to file a claim if they were lost or damaged (like that hand-painted ceramic mug that Junior made for you in preschool or all those family photo albums).

FINAL WALK-THROUGH

The day before closing, stroll through the home that will soon be yours. Take a deep breath. Feel proud. And then, look carefully around. The final walk-through provides your last chance to make sure the home is clean and all requested repairs have been made. If by some chance something is left undone, let your agent know immediately so he or she can negotiate it with the seller's agent—for example, by leaving some money in the escrow account to cover the repair cost. Please note that a final walk-through is not always part of a typical real estate transaction. We recommend it as a great way to avoid problems and relieve worry. Your agent will have to request this from the sellers and possibly make it a condition of your contract.

But even if the home is sparkling and the repairs look impeccable, make sure you get documentation stating that the repairs have been completed, as well as who did the actual work. First of all, your insurance or home warranty company may require documentation of the repairs at some point. In addition, even the best contractors occasionally slip up: if that just-repaired pipe springs another leak two weeks after closing, you need to know who can fix the problem. This is also the ideal time to get all the detailed information you'll need as the home's new owner, such as security access codes, garage door openers, and appliance manuals.

SURVIVING SETBACKS

No matter how careful you and your team have been, deals do fall apart at the last minute, even at the closing table. So, don't be shocked if a glitch occurs and has to be ironed out at the last minute before you can close. This happens all the time. Murphy's Law—a famous adage that states that whatever can go wrong, will go wrong—comes into play more often than not when it's closing time. Just be patient and things should fall into place. After all, there are so many documents and people involved in a closing—so many moving parts that something, somewhere can stop the whole machine . . . Temporarily.

If something does stall the closing, that's all it usually is: stalled. Things should be rectified in a few hours or days. However, sometimes deals do fall apart for many reasons. This can feel devastating. So much work, so much effort, so much preparation—all for nothing.

But it's not all for nothing. Having a deal fall apart is a setback and a disappointment, to be sure. But even if you have to search for a different home, much of the work is already behind you—you've received a solid market education. You know what you're looking for. You know a good inspector, a good lender, and a good agent. So, you've got a whole team already in place the moment you're ready to dust yourself off and get back on track.

CLOSING DAY

We can accurately say that closing day is a life-changing event: you walk in a renter and walk out a home owner. Whatever you feel the morning you wake up to close, there's one thing you can count on: you're prepared. "By the time I

Questions to Ask in the Final Walk-Through

1. Is the house clean and are the seller's possessions removed?
   If not, when will they be?
2. Are all the required repairs made? Did you request and receive documentation of when repairs were made and who made them?
3. Do you have all the items needed for the house (codes, openers, manuals, and warranty information, among others)?
   If not, when will you receive them?

got to closing, I had learned so much about escrow, points, real estate taxes, and everything else that it didn't matter to me that the closing itself was pretty much a mystery," remembers buyer Tonja Pitzer. "I had someone I trusted guiding me through, saying, 'Sign here, sign here.'"

On closing day, you can expect to sit at a table with a bunch of pens and sign your name so many times you start to feel like Captain Kirk at a Star Trek convention. Other than that, the procedures vary dramatically from province to province, state to state, and even city to city. The settlement agent, who runs the show, may be an attorney, a representative of a title company, or someone else entirely. You may be sitting across the table from the seller, or you may be all the way across town. Your agent or a member of the agent's team may attend to explain any last-minute questions. In any case, the settlement agent can usually explain everything as you sign documents that do the following:

1.   Finalize your mortgage.

2.   Pay the seller.

3.   Pay your closing costs.

4.   Transfer the title from the seller to you.

5.   Make arrangements to legally record the transaction

You might get the keys immediately, or it might take place only after the funds clear and the transaction is legally recorded. And, it's possible there may be a hiccup or two—Becky Pastner's husband, for example, forgot to sign his middle name on one of the forms, and the lender had to correct the error before the couple could get their home keys. But as long as you have clear expectations and follow directions, closing should be a momentous conclusion to your home-searching process and commencement of your home-owning experience.

CLOSING NIGHT

And then, suddenly, it's all over. You're no longer a renter. You're no longer a home seeker or a home buyer. You're a home owner building up equity, enjoying tax benefits, and reveling in the freedom to paint your dining room any old color you please.

Home ownership is a source of pride, contentment, and security. It does, however, come with responsibilities. Some of them are fun responsibilities, such as sprucing up the yard. Others, we must admit, can be a hassle, such as dealing with the first maintenance emergency. Fortunately, the relationship you've built with your agent doesn't end the day the deal closes. Full-service agents pride themselves in being there to answer your questions, look out for your needs, and provide service for a lifetime. Chapter 8 offers some ideas on how to take advantage of this opportunity.

What Happens to Your Mortgage After Closing Day

After closing your loan, your lender will almost certainly sell it to another company for servicing. This shouldn't worry you—it won't affect your loan or interest rate. At most, it might mean you send your payments to a different address.

However, at some point you may also decide to swap out your mortgage for a new one through refinancing, a great way to get a better interest rate, either because interest rates have fallen or because your credit score has improved.

Just remember, refinancing means you restart the clock toward payoff—although a lender can set you up with a shorter payment schedule—with a new loan and incur a new set of closing costs. If you're considering refinancing after only a couple of years, remember there are costs involved. Be sure to calculate these costs and weigh them against your anticipated savings.

Notes to Take Home

- Your preclosing responsibilities include:
  1. Staying in control of your finances
  2. Returning all phone calls and paperwork promptly
  3. Communicating with your agent at least once a week
  4. Verifying with your lender that all mortgage funding steps are completed

- Conduct a final walk-through of the home with your agent.

- Be sure you know the time and place for closing.

- Confirm with your agent that you have the following lined up and ready to go:
  1. Settlement statement—the final, official rendering of the terms of your loan and your exact closing costs
  2. Certified funds—the exact dollar amount you'll need for closing in the form of a cashier's check or other guaranteed funds
  3. Evidence of insurance—proof that you have secured your home owner's insurance, which comes in the form of an "evidence of insurance" letter from your company
  4. Clear title and title insurance—protection from liens, encumbrances, and potential costs arising from disputed ownership or faulty survey interpretation

SHARON'S FIRST HOME

"You can't afford it." That's the first thing my mother said when my husband and I told her about the plans to buy our first home. My dad, on the other hand, caved in as soon as he saw the size of the big garage. He promptly brought his boat over.

I can't say I blame my mother for being nervous. We were very young and newly married—both of us full-time students and part-time employees. But my husband and I thought buying that house made perfect sense. First, it was located in the area where we had grown up, Galena Park, Texas, where we knew everyone. Second, the asking price of $18,000 sure seemed like a sweet deal. We would be making payments on a home of our own for a little more than our monthly rent.

I smile now reflecting on that twenty-one-year-old moving into her first home. She instantly felt so mature and domesticated. All the women in both of our families had gardens and did their own pickling and canning. So I eagerly followed in their footsteps, using the home's ancient kitchen stove that came with the house to make fig preserves and jams. I can still remember the preserves bubbling in a cooking pot and the heat from that stove during those long Texas summers. My husband, meanwhile, fixed my father's boat, moved it out, and put that two-car garage to good use on various other projects. He even overhauled one of the engines of our cars.

We had so much fun in that house. It had beautiful trees in the backyard and was close to everything, including our families and childhood friends. Looking back, it seems we had parties and get-togethers almost every week. When we sold it three years later to build a home and start our family, we even made a small profit!

Home ownership has always been important in my family. Growing up during the Depression, my parents firmly believed that as long as you owned your own property—with room enough for a small garden—you'd be secure.

When my daughter was twenty, I relived the thrill of first-time home ownership by helping her buy her first home. She found a nice little place, and we helped her finance it for fifteen years, which means that by the time she's thirty-five she'll own it free and clear.

I loved being able to help my child live the American dream. I also have the satisfaction of knowing that no matter what might happen, she will always have a home. In a sense I'm passing the advice my parents gave to me—the importance of home ownership—to the next generation.

Sharon Gibbons is vice president of the MCA Division at Keller Williams Realty International.

CHAPTER 8:
PROTECT YOUR INVESTMENT

· · · · ·

Dawn Vaughn distinctly remembers the first time she walked through her home as its owner. She remembers the feeling of finally claiming as hers that 1.7-acre lot, the huge bay window in the kitchen, the wraparound deck, and the nicely finished basement. But most of all, she says, she remembers the pride.

"We brought my husband's father, uncle, and sister with us, and I remember just feeling proud," she says. "I was proud to own it, proud to show it off, and proud that we had bought such a nice house."

You don't need a book to tell you that the day you finally move into your own home will be one of the most exciting of your life. It's a major accomplishment, and something to celebrate. In fact, the thrill can persist—as long as you live in your home, you'll still feel a surge of pride every time someone admires your garden or compliments your decor.

We believe pride of ownership is only one of the ways your life will change as a home owner. Your new home comes with new privileges but also with new responsibilities. Some, like home maintenance, may seem a little confusing at first. Don't worry—like every stage you went through in the home-buying process, you'll learn to make the most of your home one step at a time. And like the rest of the process, you'll always have your agent just a phone call away and ready to offer advice and opinions even long after the deal has closed.

SERVICE FOR A LIFETIME

When you were getting started on your home-buying adventure, you carefully selected an agent who values professionalism and who builds a business on stable relationships. Over the past few weeks or months, you've probably spent a lot of time together and gotten to know each other fairly well. There's no reason to throw all that trust and rapport out the window just because the deal has closed. In fact, your agent wants you to keep in touch.

"We tell buyers that we want to be the person they go to for everything," says agent Janet Faulk in North Carolina. "We have a wealth of information, and we want to continue to share that with our buyers, no matter how long it's been since closing." Agents call this commitment "service for a lifetime," and it's especially useful in that first exciting—and surprising—year of owning your home.

You also may be surprised by how much you learn in the weeks and months after closing. There are all those things—such as a lawnmower or drill—that you probably didn't think about needing. There's that first maintenance emergency—a hassle, but you'll get through it. There may even be surprises in your own life, such as an unexpected pregnancy that suddenly makes your perfect 2/1 (two-bedroom one-bath) home a little less perfect, or a thrilling new job opportunity that changes your carefully chosen commute route.

However you decide to react to the surprises life holds, your agent will be happy to provide expertise and advice. You, too, can prepare for many surprises by becoming knowledgeable about your home's systems, quirks, and needs.

GOOD HOME HABITS

Part of the joy of owning your own home is being able to make it look exactly how you want it to look and keeping it in top condition. It's true that remembering to clean the gutters or change the air filters isn't nearly as exciting as putting a dashing new coat of paint on the living room walls. However, attention to your home's maintenance needs—even if you never so much as pick up a screwdriver yourself—is essential to protecting the long-term value of your investment.

Home maintenance falls into two main categories, which we'll call "keeping it clean," and "keeping an eye on it." First, the major systems in your home need regular maintenance, much like the oil needs to be changed in your car. Some things you can easily do yourself, like cleaning the gutters. However, some systems do best with regular attention by a professional, particularly your heating and air-conditioning systems. So, after you're settled into your home and the boxes are unpacked, we encourage you to review the maintenance needs of your home's systems and come up with a plan for regular service. This kind of maintenance not only helps prevent major disasters, it also ensures your systems will be covered by your home warranty when they do break.

In addition, smart home owners watch for new stains, cracks, peeling, or other warning signs that damage may be imminent. For example, deteriorating caulk

GOOD HOME HABITS

Keeping It Clean

Perform routine maintenance on your home's systems, depending on their age and style.

In general, your list should include the following:

1. Clean your gutters once a year.
2. Change your air filters every two to three months or when they appear dirty.
3. Have your heating and air conditioning professionally serviced once a year.
4. Change the batteries in your smoke detector once a year.
5. Read your appliance manuals for recommended upkeep, such as changing your refrigerator's water filter.

Keeping An Eye On It

Watch for signs of leaks, damage, and wear. Fixing small problems early can save you big money later.

Items to be aware of include:

1. Cracks in the ceiling or walls could indicate foundation problems.
2. Water stains indicate leaks, which need to be fixed as soon as possible.
3. Eroding caulk around doors and windows can let in moisture that causes dangerous mold growth inside your walls.
4. Buckling or faded shingles indicate your roof is nearing the end of its life.
5. Tree branches scraping your roof can damage shingles and allow pests access to your home.
6. Signs of pests common to your area.

around windows doesn't seem like a big deal, but it's one of the major culprits in mold growth. Noticing these problems sooner rather than later can keep a small problem from developing into a big one or causing a second problem. Fixing a leak in the plumbing, for example, is nothing compared to fixing the leak plus a year or two of moisture damage to your flooring or walls. Or at its most dramatic, imagine the difference a fresh pair of batteries makes in the smoke detector!

Keeping up with your home maintenance requires a little attentiveness, knowledge, and money. You can stay on top of these requirements by utilizing your home warranty and by keeping maintenance cash reserves. "As a home owner, you need to consider that maintenance or neglect will be reflected in your future selling price. If you maintain your home well, and take care of the landscaping, then you're setting yourself up for success when it comes time to sell," says Canadian agent Sylvie Begin.

Getting the Most Out of Home Warranties

Home warranties are increasingly popular deal-sweeteners for many buyers. Even if you didn't get one from the seller, you can buy one for yourself. If the seller chose the policy, you can usually make changes to what is covered within the first month of owning your home. Be sure to read the fine print—most policies exclude certain appliances or systems, so you may be in for a surprise if you find out the refrigerator is not covered only after it goes warm. And, we suggest you make any changes as soon as possible. Warranty companies don't want you to wait for the water heater to break and then add it to your coverage if it wasn't originally covered, so they usually require a technician to certify its condition (at your cost) if you want to add coverage further down the road.

In order to get the most out of your home warranty, we want you to make sure you understand what might cause the warranty company to deny coverage. Some companies use poor maintenance as a reason for denial. Others may not cover repairs that were reviewed by someone the warranty provider didn't send. For example, if your air conditioner dies and you ask Joe, the HVAC technician next door, to look at it before you call the warranty company, coverage might be denied.

Warranties cost several hundred dollars annually, so many buyers, especially ones with new homes, decide their money would be better spent making repairs themselves. But those who have had warranties cover a several-thousand-dollar job often swear by their long-term value.

"I bought my home two years ago, and within four months I started having AC problems," says agent Carol Peyton. "My home warranty replaced both my compressors for the fifty-five dollar trip charge. So I think they're worth it. It does depend on the age of the home, but I've always continued my warranty."

Maintenance Reserves

Whether or not you have a warranty, you should definitely have a maintenance budget. Depending on the size and age of your home, you can expect to spend several hundred to several thousand dollars on maintenance each year. Budgeting for these costs will ease the crunch in an emergency, and it will also help you stay on top of seemingly minor problems that can grow exponentially worse over time. Even if you don't end up spending all your reserves, you can always use the cash for fun home-improvement projects, such as retiling the bathroom or landscaping the backyard.

In the end, the responsibilities that come with owning a home are dwarfed by the joys and privileges of home ownership. The last step in your home-buying process should be obvious—celebrate your achievement.

CELEBRATE!

You've finally made it to the end of your home-buying journey and to the beginning of life as a home owner. Different people celebrate this accomplishment in different ways. Some people throw a big party to meet all their new neighbors. Some people go on a painting blitz or plant a half-dozen new trees. Some people just want to sit on the couch, gaze admiringly at the walls and the ceiling, and feel all tingly. And for many owners, one of the most fulfilling ways to celebrate the opportunity and privilege of owning their own homes is by getting involved in their neighborhoods.

After all, it's natural that when you're putting down roots, you start thinking about ways to improve the soil. As people settle into the neighborhoods they expect to call home for years, many home owners find their new commitment makes them think about their community in a new way. They find that pretty soon, their commitment extends beyond their four walls and into making their neighborhood the best it can be. They help in many ways—from cleaning up parks to buying cookies from the Girl Scouts, to serving as precinct captains for their political party, to volunteering in their churches, synagogues, and mosques. Whatever form it takes, many home owners find that the connection between owning a home they care about, and caring about the people outside their home, brings the benefits of ownership to a whole new level.

We wish you the best in making the most of your new home and filling it with good moments and lasting memories. This is something Datri Gasser thinks about as she slowly updates the gracious 1920s home she bought in Seattle, Washington. The previous owner, an elderly woman named Marjorie, lived there for fifty-three years—nearly as long as Wini and Stanley lived in their little Cape Cod home in Levittown. In that time Marjorie had taken exquisite care of her home, filling it with the relics of a half a century of living. Datri has no plans to stay put nearly as long, but as she looks toward the years ahead she still feels a sense of permanence. "We have a deep respect for our house because Marjorie took such good care of it," she says. "We want to do the same, to take care of it and appreciate it, and then pass it on to someone else." Although Datri and her husband have lived in their home for several years, the excitement of owning it never seems to wear off. "We felt so lucky when we bought our home," says Datri. "We still feel lucky every day."

Onward

We hope you've enjoyed reading this book as much as we enjoyed putting it together. The purchase of your first home represents a huge step in the direction of growth and responsibility in your life. But we want you to consider something else. Buying your first home is also a huge step in your financial maturity; it's an investment that lays the groundwork for financial well-being for the rest of your life.

Think about it this way. Chances are good that the home you buy will not be your last. In fact, across North America the average home owner moves about every six or seven years. So, what does that mean for you? It means the potential for selling in the future and moving into a new, better home—maybe even your dream home. It could also mean buying a second property, and keeping your first home as a rental property, which can provide passive income for a lifetime.

If you choose to stay and live in your first home for a long period of time, at the very least, you can tap into your home equity for making improvements and increasing the value of your home. Any way you look at it, your first home means financial possibilities and long-term security for you and your family. We're excited for you, and we wish you the best in your home-buying, and ultimately, wealth-building journey.

Notes to Take Home

- After closing your agent can still help you with such things as providing information for your tax returns, finding contractors and repair services, and even tracking your home's current market value.

- Perform routine maintenance on your home's systems, and seek professional attention when necessary.

- Watch for signs of leaks, damage, and wear. Fixing small problems early will save you big money later.

- Take pride in home ownership and enjoy its benefits.

EVERYONE DESERVES TO OWN A HOME

We believe everyone deserves a chance to fulfill the dream of owning a home, especially those families whose economic circumstances make it seem impossible.

It's hard to imagine, but each year millions of people across the United States and Canada experience homelessness or a lack of access to affordable, adequate housing. Among those affected include the elderly, military veterans, and families. Even more unsettling is the fact that children are likely to make up a third of the homeless population in a typical year—with more than one million in the United States alone.

For these reasons, the authors will donate a portion of the proceeds from every sale of this book to charitable organizations working to eliminate homelessness and provide adequate housing to all those in need. Please visit YourFirstHomeBook.com for more information.

INDEX

. . . . .